MAKING THE MONEY SING

MAKING THE MONEY SING

Private Wealth and Public Power in the Search for Peace

JOHN TIRMAN

ROWMAN & LITTLEFIELD PUBLISHERS, INC.
Lanham • Boulder • New York • Oxford

ROWMAN & LITTLEFIELD PUBLISHERS, INC.

Published in the United States of America
by Rowman & Littlefield Publishers, Inc.
4720 Boston Way, Lanham, Maryland 20706
http://www.rowmanlittlefield.com

12 Hid's Copse Road
Cumnor Hill, Oxford OX2 9JJ, England

British Library Cataloging in Publication Information Available

Library of Congress Cataloging-in-Publication Data
Tirman, John.
    Making the money sing : private wealth and public power in the
search for peace / John Tirman.
    p. cm.
        Includes bibliographical references and index.
        ISBN 0-8476-9922-6
        1. Peace movements. 2. Antinuclear movement. 3. Endowments. I.
Title.
JZ5574 .T57 2000
327.1'72—dc21

                                                              00-033269

Printed in the United States of America

♾™ The paper used in this publication meets the minimum
requirements of American National Standard for Information Sciences—
Permanence of Paper for Printed Library Materials, ANSI/NISO Z39.48-
1992.

To the life, work, and achievements of
Robert Winston Scrivner

CONTENTS

FOREWORD

This book chronicles a pivotal period in the history of philanthropy—one that saw charitable funds marshaled in support of not only political goals, but also of the political processes by which those goals might be achieved. Global politics during this period, from the early 1980s to the late 1990s, ranged from the stable hostility of the Cold War to the surprising instability of the post–Cold War world. The importance of what John Tirman has accomplished in this book starts with the fact that, even among many of those who played active roles in the story he tells, no synthesizing view of the history seems to be well understood. But there is more to say.

The original idea behind this book was to recount the work of the Winston Foundation for World Peace over its brief existence from 1985 to 1999. John was our one and only executive director. Wanting some record of our work, it seemed a good idea for him to to keep track of it. As you will discover, however, a simple show-and-tell of Winston's accomplishments was not in the end what John did. Instead, he has written an important historical account that brings Winston's work into the picture where appropriate but only to add texture to the much broader story that he has pieced together from many disparate events. While his conclusions may strike some as debatable, he supports them with a persuasive assembling of facts. And there are none of those pious claims of unproven and unprovable achievement by the firm of which he is a part.

John dedicates this book to Bob Scrivner, whose intellectual and monetary capital launched Winston and guided its work throughout. What should be noted is the uncommon investment skill, generosity, and commitment to peace that made common cause in Bob's life, enabling the work of Winston to be launched following his death in 1984. Bob was in partnership with an investment firm specializing in futures. While distinguishing himself in the world of philanthropy by day, his nights were often spent developing the trading programs that made his investment firm one of the very best in its arcane field of futures trading in commodities, currencies, and financial instruments. The quality of this work earned praise from his partners and a fortune for the firm. It was his share of this fortune that he dedicated to Winston. So grateful for his skilled programming and impressed with his purposes in founding Winston were his partners at the investment firm, that for the first seven years of Winston's operations, the head of the firm matched, dollar for dollar, every Winston grant, thereby doubling its effectiveness.

In sum, Winston was thrice blessed: to have Bob Scrivner as its founder and spiritual leader, to have the abundant support of Bob's professional colleagues and, from start to finish, to have John Tirman at the helm as its executive director.

Bevis Longstreth
President of Winston Foundation for World Peace

PREFACE AND ACKNOWLEDGMENTS

This book is the story of how a few dozen people, with access to money, tried to alter the landscape of global politics, and achieved much more than most of them probably dreamed. It is also the story about how the lessons of that singular experience—the movement to end the nuclear arms race in the 1980s—was not fully appreciated or absorbed. It is an extraordinary tale that has never before been told.

It is also a tale of how the deployment of enormous private wealth—the accumulated fortunes of Rockefeller and Ford, Turner and Soros—is wielded on behalf of the great issues of war and peace. Private philanthropy is largely an American phenomenon, and while donors, whether public or private, tend to work in similar ways, those with their own wealth are likely to be more inventive, capricious, and take more risks than those hemmed in by the rules and procedures of the modern bureaucracy. Vast sums are too often wasted or misused, regrettably, but such money is sometimes maneuvered cleverly to foment remarkable change. That tale is too little told and is rarely told well.

Finally, this book is a story about the tests confronting these wealthy few in the post–Cold War world. The twentieth century—which encapsulates the birth and growth of the great philanthropic foundations—endured numerous cataclysmic changes, among them was the sudden escalation of the U.S.–Soviet rivalry in the early 1980s, and then its equally sudden demise. Naturally, this rise and fall of superpower tension was at the core of concern among donors in international affairs. But the aftermath, the decade of the 1990s, became a perplexing snarl of ethnic conflict, failed states, wrenching globalization, and an America globally more dominant than ever while increasingly detached from the world beyond its shores. Breaking through that detachment, and, more importantly, finding ways to stop the rampaging violence across the globe now appear as the primary challenges to internationalists. Nothing less than creating a more stable, just, and peaceful world is the central aspiration of the donors, and the activists and scholars they support. In some ways, this new agenda is even more outrageously ambitious than the one derided as quixotic just a decade before—that is, reversing the nuclear arms race and ending the Cold War.

I was an accidental tourist of sorts in these adventures, the executive director of the Winston Foundation for World Peace from 1986 through 1999. It was my good fortune to be present during much of this history, having been on the senior staff of one of the key advocacy groups, the Union of Concerned Scientists, from 1982 to1986, and an observer and sometimes chronicler of these movements before then. I also advised two other philanthropies between 1989 and 1994, so my perspective was perhaps broader than most. I set out to write this book mainly as a short history of the Winston Foundation, and discovered that there was this much bigger story to convey, a drama in which the Winston Foundation, like several other funders, played a significant part.

The foundation itself was the creation of one of the legends of philanthropy, Robert Winston Scrivner, who was a longtime adviser to the Rockefeller family in its generous and visionary giving. He was executive director of the Rockefeller Family Fund for twelve years until his death, at the age of forty-eight, in 1984. As is described in the following pages, his leadership in the donor community, particularly in the burgeoning antinuclear movement of the early 1980s, is one of the outstanding examples of risk-taking, "entrepreneurial" philanthropy.

It was his spirit and philosophy of grant making that we tried to emulate at the Winston Foundation, aided considerably by the people he asked to serve on the board. The ten original trustees remained active in the life of the foundation throughout its fifteen years: John Adams, Robert Allen, Roy Carlin, Leslie Dunbar, Alice Tepper Marlin, Karl Mathiasen, Melinda B. Scrivner, Albert G. Sims, William D. Zabel, and the board president, Bevis Longstreth. This exceptional group of individuals—all friends or family or professional colleagues of Bob Scrivner—was not only a thoughtful and caring board, but it also played several roles outside the Winston sphere that were profoundly important to the story I describe. They were joined in 1996 by new trustees Eliza Klose and Susan Collin Marks, two equally gifted and dedicated people. This was the kind of talent pool any executive director would yearn for.

While we tried to be venturesome and visionary, the results were not always what we hoped for. This is the nature of philanthropy, especially in a broad, public policy endeavor like global peace. There are many more failures in one's grant making than successes. The story I describe about peace philanthropy, and the critiques I offer of errant strategies or sometimes worse, should not imply that I believe we always made the right choices. We made—I made—plenty of mistakes.

But the work we undertook was always intended to lower superpower tensions and enhance the prospects for disarmament, and then, in the 1990s, to invest in the growth of civil society organizations that were building constituencies and tools for the permanent prevention of conflict. In this, I am confident, we broadly made the right decisions and contributed to some concrete achievements.

We were aided by staff people of uncommon skills and commitment. Two in particular were central to the Winston story and do not receive as much attention in the following pages as they deserve: Nancy Stockford, who served with me for ten years starting at the Union of Concerned Scientists in 1983, and Tara Magner, who succeeded her at the foundation and stayed on to the conclusion of our work in late 1999. These are distinguished professionals and valued friends. We also benefitted by the hard work of several other colleagues, most prominently Monica Dorbandt, Jean Donnelly Linde, and Bill Parsons. In researching this book, I had very useful assistance from Matt Fellowes. I would also like to thank the people who allowed me to interview them. As a side note, all quotations in this book that are not footnoted have come from one of these interviews conducted between July 1999 and November 1999. Although most quotes are attributed to the individual, in a few cases, the interviewee asked not to be identified.

I dedicate this book to Bob Scrivner, whom I never knew, but I have worked closely with his widow, Melinda, and I bring special recognition to her singular contributions to the Winston effort. Her own idealism, enthusiasm, collaborative spirit, and personal encouragement were absolutely pivotal in the foundation's endeavors. I also wish to pay tribute here to three men—remarkable men in their intellect, their insights, their teamwork, and their indefatigable work for peace—I knew well who have passed on: Ping Ferry, Henry Kendall, and Peter Clausen. I also honor my late father, Wallace S. Tirman, M.D., whose own dedication to the well being of ordinary people has always been for me a guiding principle of action.

I have benefitted greatly from the love and support of my extraordinary partner and wife, Nike Zachmanoglou, who has unfailingly encouraged and enabled my work. I wrote this book while we began our greatest adventure, the raising of our little girl, Coco, and, as a result, I will always associate these pages with the pleasures of fatherhood. It once struck me as mawkish, but now seems obvious to say that it is for her generation and those following that I hope the work of the Winston Foundation makes a more peaceful world.

1

PRIVATE WEALTH
AND PUBLIC ASPIRATIONS

The great enterprise of American philanthropy has evoked a cloud of mystery about it, an aura of enigmatic power derived from its majestic wealth and cloistered ways. While its size is much smaller and its unity of purpose less coherent than government or business, philanthropy is often seen as possessing a matchless ability to affect society, for good or ill. The colossal growth in affluence in the United States since the early 1980s, and the gradual transfer of wealth from the World War II generation to daughters and sons and grandchildren, fortify the hunch that the world of philanthropy is more muscular and forceful than ever. No less a social critic than Nicholas Lemann asserted in 1997 a "shift in power from government to foundations." Philanthropic endeavors, he said, have none of "the large, demanding constituencies that other kinds of institutions must keep informed and happy: they have no voters, no customers, no investors. The press, which pays close attention to politics and government through deeply ingrained reflex, largely ignores foundations, or treats them, in a polite but faintly bored tone, as innocuous do-gooders rather than significant actors." Foundations, he concluded, "deserve to be brought into the company of central institutions whose course is the subject of constant public scrutiny and debate." Hear, hear.

To the extent such debate occurs, however, it is either exceptionally narrow—about tax status or spending levels—or extremely partisan, fodder for old-fashioned diatribes from the left or right wings or even conspiracy yarns.[1] More ink is given to the rare scandals in the world of philanthropy and the "will he or won't he" speculations about Bill Gates or Warren Buffet than the prosaic reality of grant making to the tens of thousands of social service providers and public interest groups that is the daily routine of foundation officers.

Still, foundations do have the power to foment change, to transform issues of public concern or neglect, and in this they are significant

1

players in the life of America. There is, moreover, both a penchant for secrecy—or, at least, a habit of keeping cards close to the chest—and a stuffy self-importance, derived from the peculiarity of spending other people's money. These features seem especially true of grant makers interested in foreign affairs, an elevated plateau on the philanthropic terrain that for several decades appeared to be far from the pedestrian worries of the masses. But what is most remarkable about philanthropy in this field is neither the secrecy nor the political leverage, but the unexamined goals and outcomes of the billions of dollars expended. So much has been poured into what can only be described as an endorsement of the status quo. The very idea of foundations being agents of social change—of trying to promote, for example, a durable peace independent of government or business interests—was, in this secluded aerie, a wholly laughable notion until about two decades ago.

THE NEW PHILANTHROPY OF DISARMAMENT

For most of its history, American philanthropy approached foreign policy gingerly, typically supporting no more than the major research institutes and elite clubs. This support reflected in part society's attitude—foreign affairs were for the "striped pants set," the diplomats and Wall Street lawyers and tweedy professors. A handful of foundations underwrote the studies, monographs, and conferences of this elite, and these intellectual exercises rarely wandered outside the boundaries of acceptable discourse. A few large foundations like Ford and Rockefeller donated substantial sums for Third World development, population stabilization, and the like. In this enduring tradition, the notion that American foundations might support a social and political movement aimed at disrupting long-standing security policy was unorthodox, virtually heretical. The prospect of funding transnational organizations that intended to influence other governments, especially the Soviet Union, was equally novel. If anything, foundations were viewed as adjuncts of the ponderous institutions that merely confirmed the predilections of the power elite. Executives of foundations and senior officials in government were seemingly two sides of the same coin, and the ideas and actions of philanthropy simply did not challenge the basic precepts of U.S. foreign policy, *especially* those bracing the Cold War.

By 1980, this prim custom was undergoing a drastic transformation. The spur for this change was the sudden diplomatic rupture between the superpowers. The long period of detente with Moscow had crumbled under the weight of Soviet misbehavior—the occupation of Afghanistan, in particular—and constant hammering from a newly energized political right wing in America. President Jimmy Carter, saying he had been fooled by the Russians, ordered up several new nuclear missile systems like the MX, Trident II, and Pershing II and cruise missiles for Europe. The icy chill in U.S.–USSR relations also spelled the end of the series of arms-control successes that began with the Nuclear Non-Proliferation Treaty (NPT) in the late 1960s, and included the Strategic Arms Limitation Treaties (SALT I and II) and the Anti-Ballistic Missile (ABM) Treaty. With the election of Ronald Reagan and the searing, truculent bravado that accompanied his victory, the Cold War was descending into a darker phase. In view of the ruinous firepower of the two adversaries' nuclear arsenals—many times greater than the last testy period in the early 1960s—a frightening sense of danger was palpable.

This nuclear danger drove several leaders of small foundations to search for a new way of affecting the policy-making apparatus in Washington. Clearly, the polite discussion of the Council on Foreign Relations or the Brookings Institution was unlikely to stop this careening juggernaut of the renewed Cold War. Something more public, and far more confrontational, was required. These donors, many of whom had been meeting regularly at informal lunches in New York to discuss such issues, did not have the grant-making clout of Ford or Rockefeller, but they did have a sense that small amounts of money could catalyze a strong and insistent protest throughout America.

Their hunch was not conjured in a vacuum. A grassroots movement was forming, drawing organizers from previous campaigns such as the Clamshell Alliance, the antinuclear power protestors, and the residue of antiwar activists of the Vietnam War period. Durable, church-based groups like the American Friends Service Committee, the action arm of the Quakers, and the Fellowship of Reconciliation were mounting projects against the arms race, as were some other organizations like the Council for a Livable World that had hibernated through much of the 1970s. But a new force was also rising, and rising quickly— the Nuclear Weapons Freeze Campaign, created via the simple proposal by a Massachusetts Institute of Technology grad student, Randy Forsberg, and a coterie of peace activists in western Massachusetts that called for the end of all production and deployment of nuclear weapons. A parallel, anti-intervention movement was also rapidly growing in response to Reagan's particular bête noire, the Marxist insurgency in Central America.

This small group of donors recognized the burgeoning peace movement as an opportunity to contend with the resurgent right and to bypass the inert discourse of the elite institutions of New York and Washington. Confronting the nuclear arms race would mean confronting the way foreign policy decisions were made, another departure from the old philanthropy. But the danger was so menacing, so proximate in the rhetoric of Reagan and his cohorts, that mere argument about the policy was obviously inadequate. Instead, everything about the Cold War, from the haunting possibility of nuclear holocaust to the economic burdens of the superpower rivalry to the culture of militarism fostered in the West and East, would have to be subject to debate, protest, and reform in the cities and towns of America, right to the epicenters of the "twilight struggle" in Moscow and Washington.

The funders group included people typical of the American elite: graduates of Harvard and Princeton, lawyers and journalists, and some who were wealthy themselves. They gravitated to this cause and to each other for many varied reasons, but they had a remarkably congruous view of the danger and their requisite response. Among them were Robert Scrivner, who headed the Rockefeller Family Fund; Cora Weiss of the Samuel Rubin Foundation; David Hunter, who headed both the Ottinger Foundation and the Stern Fund; Wade Greene, an advisor to five individuals in the Rockefeller family; David Ramage of the New World Foundation; Ed Lawrence of the Veatch Program; and W. H. "Ping" Ferry, an individual donor. They were joined by others in 1981 and 1982, forming a nucleus of an activist-oriented peace donors group. By 1984, some five or six dozen foundations were funding the peace movement, including some of the largest philanthropies in the country—the Carnegie Corporation, the John D. and Catherine T. MacArthur Foundation, Rockefeller Brothers Fund, and the W. Alton Jones Foundation.

The impact of this philanthropy was powerful. The peace movement altered the national perception of the nuclear danger, mobilized millions of Americans to protest the arms race, emboldened Congress to adopt an independent course supporting arms control, and spurred dozens of political leaders around the world to insist on renewed superpower detente. How all this activity, and the philanthropy supporting it, actually contributed to the end of the Cold War is a controversial question. But the astonishing scale and persistence of the protest—among the largest movements for change in American history—are undeniable.

By the end of 1991, when the Soviet Union collapsed, the peace donors were a scattered lot. Even as some of the major successes of detente and disarmament were unfolding in the late 1980s, a number of foundations were leaving the field or reorienting their international focus. Several were drawn to domestic priorities by the slashes in federal spending on poverty programs. Others were alarmed by the long, hot summer of 1988 and the harrowing prospect of an "end of nature." But some were simply weary of the politics of protest and discouraged by a dramatic decline in the grassroots peace movement in America, a movement that quickly dissipated along with the possibility of a nuclear war. The foundations that once had acted with remarkable coherence to end the Cold War drifted onto three or four separate funding paths. Of those remaining in the field, most continued with a variation of nuclear arms control that emphasized nuclear nonproliferation. A second path led to the injurious side effects of the Cold War—high defense spending, the secrecy and bullying of the "national security state," military adventurism, and the polluted nuclear weapons complex. A third turned to the ripe notions of collective security, or newer ideas of cooperative security, believing that the United Nations and other multilateral organizations should be the locus of attention and action in international affairs. And a fourth path, the most divergent, saw new opportunities to prevent conflict in Africa, the Balkans, the Caucasus, and elsewhere, utilizing the new, robust activism within civil society the world over.

Each of these paths could lead to gratifying results. But the transformative potential in a unified group of donors was lost. The absence of a vibrant social and political movement in America also meant that donors concentrating on U.S. policy were left with the old devices of influence—studies and conferences, elite-opinion shaping, and government access. As a result, an entirely new class of elites had been added to the old institutions, the public interest think tanks and lobbying groups that grew to prominence during the last decade of the Cold War. That was no small achievement. But by 1993, this Washington complex of peace lobbyists was much more an "epistemic community"—one that aimed to improve policy rather than challenge its content and formulation—than the "critical community" that helped fuel the historic protests of the 1980s. And this reliance on the old ways of doing things, albeit with some new players, produced results in the 1990s that were dramatically less fruitful than the previous ten years. In contrast, those who supported the critical communities abroad—the civil society organizations working for an end to conflict, for the protection of human rights, and so forth—enjoyed a more promising outcome, in terms of actual transformation, if one more difficult to measure.

Here I am comparing two very distinct decades, with strikingly dissimilar concerns, dangers, leaders, and events. But philanthropy's significant impact in the 1980s should not be discounted simply because it was engineered within a unique set of historical circumstances; any given era has its unique features. What we do have are some strong indicators about what constitutes effective philanthropy, based on what we saw happen in a very fluid, changeable period that was also a time of rich engagement by American donors.

LEGENDS OF AMERICAN PHILANTHROPY

The popular view of philanthropy revolves around the doings of the super-rich—Andrew Carnegie and John D. Rockefeller Sr. at the beginning of the twentieth century, or Bill Gates, Ted Turner, and George Soros at century's end. They are seen as great industrialists (or robber barons) who repaid a kind of debt owed to the society that enabled their vast wealth; *noblesse oblige*, the obligations of nobility, is a phrase that frequently surfaces, with all its latent meanings. As exemplars, these men do deserve gratitude, and their foundations or families, particularly four generations of Rockefellers, can be counted among the best donors in America.

Philanthropy intended to alter fundamental relationships in American society and the world before the latter years of the twentieth century were scarce, but there is a tradition of sorts in social-change giving. One could start with the Tappan brothers, Arthur and Lewis, who made a fortune in the silk trade and a company that later became Dunn & Bradstreet, and then turned their attentions to the abolition of slavery. As founders of the American Anti-Slavery Society and the journal, the *Emancipator*, the Tappans employed many of the social-change tactics familiar to activists nearly two centuries later: use of news media and publicity, nonviolent public actions, legal initiatives (including the *Amistad* case), organizing within churches, and becoming involved in lobbying and electoral politics. In the 1830s, abolitionism was a radical movement, and there was danger in it for the Tappans, who had their homes trashed by mobs, among other affronts. They persisted and lived to see the Emancipation Proclamation.[2] (Contrast this remarkable activism with the comment by Carnegie Corporation president Frederick Keppel in the 1930s that he was embarrassed to have supported Gunnar Myrdal's landmark study of racial relations, *An American Dilemma*.) In the early twentieth century, another set of brothers, department store magnates Edward and Lincoln Filene, not only created and backed several innovative institutions—including the Twentieth Century Fund—but introduced a number of enlightened practices into their business, including profit sharing and health care. But these unusual men of wealth were rarities.

Andrew Carnegie is the one typically regarded as a paragon, even a sire, of American philanthropy, due to his ubiquitous gifts—public libraries, in particular, a donation promoting more social change than he probably imagined—and his powerful challenge to his contemporaries to leave all their money to charity. A commanding concern late in his life was war, the "foulest blot on our civilization," and he set out to abolish it through the creation of one of the first public interest organizations, the Carnegie Endowment for International Peace. A few years later he endowed the Carnegie Corporation of New York, which was (and is) his principal grant-making legacy. But while Carnegie himself was deeply involved and had strong feelings about war and peace—inclined, in fact, toward pacifism—he did not impart a grant-making strategy, mirroring a tendency of the other major philanthropists of the early twentieth century. In the absence of such strategic thinking, the large foundations in particular are pulled toward the irresistible force of bureaucracy to be cautious and centrist, though, of course, with strong leadership they can leave that orbit and deploy their ample resources with great effect. But the proclivity, with few exceptions, is toward the center of things. In global security issues, that has meant an unmistakable urge to be "players," to be a part of the great game of high diplomacy. In the words of one critique, these dynamics result in "foundation programs . . . designed to further the foreign policy interests of the United States."[3]

That this has been the way most philanthropies drift—those conscious of their roles as architects of public policy—was apparent even after the social and political upheavals of the 1960s. "It would be almost impossible to know from the grants in 1972," an analysis of philanthropy notes, "that a massive citizen's movement had evolved to oppose the war in Vietnam."[4] The lack of daring among most funders stirred David Hunter to challenge his counterparts in a speech before the Council on Foundations in 1975, a speech that many among progressive donors recall as a galvanizing source in the growth of social-change philanthropy.

More resources did begin to flow into social-change strategies after 1980, perhaps as a result of the Reagan presidency, though the numbers remained very modest. According to one analysis, in the mid-1980s some $253 billion was spent in the nonprofit sector (including time volunteered), of which 96 percent went to "service providers"—hospitals, homeless shelters, disaster relief, and so forth. Perhaps $200–300 million, including private donations, was invested in social change activities. (In 1999 dollars, that would be about $300–450 million.) Of that, a fraction was dedicated to international activities, perhaps one-fifth, or a total of roughly $60–90 million annually going to strategies aimed at disarmament and the like.[5] That is 0.015 percent of what flows through American philanthropy as a whole. But the numbers belie influence, in fact, and underscore how a few visionaries can leverage small amounts of money to great effect. This situation is precisely what began to happen in the late 1970s and early 1980s, under the guidance of the new legends of philanthropy, the likes of David Hunter, Robert Scrivner, Wade

Greene, and the rest. They created, in essence, a new tradition of international giving that had only occasionally appeared before, and they did not need to move mountains of money to do it.

THE PRACTICE OF CHANGING THE WORLD

The small band of funders who invested early in the 1980s to stop the arms race, whether consciously or not, were undertaking two crucial tasks. Social-change theorists see the confluence of critical communities—intellectuals, mainly, who formulate the ideas challenging the status quo—and social movements, which absorb and transform those ideas into an action agenda, as the necessary precondition of pervasive change in the public's attitudes and ultimately in politicians' actions. The social movements are crucial, not only because they create or manifest a "public demand" for change, but because they themselves are carriers of new cultural values, ideas, and principles of the political culture that nourish the roots of public demands. The intellectuals sometimes detect and sometimes stir that inchoate demand, translating it into the historical and analytical framework that appeals to the gatekeepers in the news media, educational institutions, and policy circles. "The creation of new values," writes Thomas Rochon, a leading theorist of how social change arises, "begins with the generation of new ideas or perspectives among small groups of critical thinkers: people whose experiences, reading, and interaction with each other help them to develop a set of cultural values that is out of step with the larger society. The dissemination of those values occurs through social and political movements in which the critical thinkers may participate, but whose success is determined to a far greater degree by the course of collective action in support of the new values."[6]

That "course of collective action" is the pathway forged by the grant makers and the many activists and intellectuals of the peace movement beginning at the end of the 1970s. There were, of course, earlier antinuclear movements, some quite significant in size and having important consequences, particularly the test ban movement of the early 1960s. The movement of the 1980s was more robust, however, not only because it was larger and noisier, but because it utilized a more powerful critique of the Cold War and alternatives to the nuclear rivalry that resonated widely. Both of these features—the scale and the sophistication—were significantly due to the social-change philanthropists. The funders contributed money to both the critical community and to the burgeoning social movements that were focusing their energies on the new and dangerous phase of the Cold War. Many of these donors were active participants in framing the critique, moreover, and were bridges from various clans of intellectuals to the various formations of activists. By the time the antinuclear surge was cresting, larger donors had been captivated, too, and were able to inject much larger amounts of money into each new phase of the critique and protest of the superpower rivalry.

This sometimes coordinated and intensively involved role for donors was virtually without an antecedent in the corner of American giving that addresses international issues. (The civil rights movement had had such deep involvement from donors from the 1960s, and this stirred other rights-based movements that have transformed American politics.) This camaraderie was one that lasted only fitfully for a few years. When the end of the Cold War suddenly appeared, the rough coherence of the peace donors' group dissipated. But what also declined in America, simultaneously, was that singular impetus in the political culture for change, the grassroots dynamism that so dramatically reshaped the topography of U.S. debate and action in the superpower arena. Left to their own devices, without a social movement or a relatively unified set of critical thinkers, the funders split into different directions.

In regarding Lemann's challenge from this standpoint, a decade after the Cold War ended, what is striking is not the absence of scrutiny of foundations or the teapot tempest over the comparative influence of the right or the left in philanthropy. And the notion that a noticeable shift in power to foundations from government is doubtful. What is, in my view, the far more important and interesting question is how nonprofit dollars make a difference: What are the goals, and how do we—as philanthropists, researchers, and activists—achieve them? The answer to this question is not only the Rosetta stone of philanthropy, it should be its moral guide as well.

2

THE EARLY PEACE DONORS

"We had an office, a walk-up off an alleyway, and lo and behold, one day we get a visit from the executive director of the Rockefeller Family Fund, Bob Scrivner. We'd never seen a foundation executive before. He came and spoke with us and talked about the strategy and politics of nuclear disarmament. He was thoughtful and well-read. It was a remarkable experience."[1] That recollection, by one of the early activists of the burgeoning effort to end the nuclear arms race, captures perfectly the spirit of engagement, not just of Bob Scrivner, but of about a dozen donors of this new social movement. In foreign policy circles, it was an unprecedented form of involvement, in an area that had long been neglected by traditional philanthropy. Social movements were not new, of course, and philanthropy had been involved in some. But the field of international security—particularly the arena of nuclear decision making—had been off-limits to foundations, a self-imposed exile. That was to change in the blink of an eye in the late 1970s, and with it the entire edifice of the nuclear enterprise.

THE PIONEERS

A loosely knit collection of private donors began to meet in New York to discuss nuclear issues and related matters in the 1970s. The "ringleader," most agree, was David Hunter, a Texas-born social worker who was shaped into an internationalist by his post–World War II experience with the strategic bombing survey in Europe. He returned to work first for the United Nations International Children's Emergency Fund (UNICEF) and then at the Ford Foundation. "We rode herd on youth development, but there wasn't much interest in peace movement issues at Ford," he recalls. He went to work for Phil Stern at his family's philanthropy, and managed it and a few other small foundations over the ensuing twenty years. Hunter quickly came to be recognized as an innovator in philanthropy, exhorting his colleagues to invest in social change. "We didn't shy away from people and groups who frightened some other people," he says of his funding outlook. "Looking over the territory of good things to do to save the world, we tried to find organizations that had some special energy." When the good times of U.S.–USSR relations began to come apart in the late 1970s, David Hunter saw a need and opportunity to address the causes and consequences of the Cold War.

"A few of us started a little discussion group on peace issues in the 1970s, David Hunter, Phil Stern, Sidney Shapiro, and myself. We met for lunch, maybe once a month, at David's club," recalls Cora Weiss, president of the Samuel Rubin Foundation. "Later, Anne Zill, Carol Guyer, and some others joined in. We did a Soviet-American conference at the Century Association, which was considered very *avant garde*. There was also a meeting of progressive donors at Cold Spring Harbor, and I remember saying to them, 'I don't care what you do, what you fund, but please do just one thing for peace.'"

Cora Weiss was one of those people who seemed to be central to every moment of peace politics since the early 1960s. Her father, Sam Rubin, was a funder of the civil rights movement and bequeathed enough to the foundation that bears his name to be an important, if small, donor in the life of many peace and justice organizations. Cora was a prominent peace activist in her own right as a major antiwar player during the Vietnam War period. "It wasn't easy to raise money in those days," she recalls. "I plumbed Sterling Grumman and Dan Bernstein and Stewart Mott for contributions. Funders were not used to putting money into demonstrations. Too political. I actually raised money at protests with a tin can. By the late 1970s, it was no different. Organized philanthropy was slow and scared and traditional."

The helicopters lifting the last Americans off the rooftop of the embassy in Saigon was a recent memory when the edgy, new concern about nuclear weapons was surfacing among the progressive donors on the East Coast. Sidney Shapiro at the Levinson Foundation in Boston, Phil Stern, David Hunter, and Cora were cohorts from the earlier campaigns for civil rights and an end to the U.S. intervention in Vietnam. Anne Zill of the Stewart Mott office and Carol Guyer of the J. C. Penney Foundation were among the additions when the informal group gradually expanded to include Bob Scrivner, Wade Greene, W. H. "Ping" Ferry, Ed Lawrence, and David Ramage. Greene, a former writer and editor with *Newsweek* and the *New York Times*, advised five cousins of the Rockefeller family on their personal philanthropy. Ping Ferry was a leading intellectual, long a colleague of Robert Hutchins at the Center for the Study of Democratic Institutions, and by the late 1970s a private donor. Ed Lawrence, an engineer, ran the Veatch Program, created by a Unitarian church on Long Island that was bequeathed a natural gas field in Germany. David Ramage, president of the New World Foundation in New York, was a theologian who later headed a Chicago seminary. There were others, too, in and out of the discussions of those early years—Leslie Dunbar and Dick Boone of the Field Foundation, a philanthropy derived from the Chicago department-store fortune; John A. Harris IV, a private donor whose family built wealth in the oil business; and Robert Allen of the Kendall Foundation in Boston.

Each of them shared a driving concern about the actual possibility of a nuclear war. Another impetus for involvement, in equal measure if not evenly shared, was the opening to confront the militarization of American politics and society. What this small group with relatively small resources did, however, was utterly remarkable: It stirred a broad, new social movement to end the nuclear arms race.

"Concern for nuclear war moved my sources and other donors, too," says Wade Greene. "That's what people were worried about. Yes, we had lots of meetings, and some of the discussions were quite emotional—you know, with visions of nuclear bombs going off. There was a sense that we really were going to blow each other up."

"I was more concerned about militarization," remembers David Hunter. "I guess I thought that we wouldn't let a nuclear war happen. You had to try to prevent it whether you thought it would happen or not."

For several philanthropies, the focus on nuclear weapons was a natural extension of their work on nuclear power. In the late 1970s, the expanding industry producing nuclear-generated electricity was a target of a sizable social movement. The safety of nuclear reactors had come under sharp criticism by the Union of Concerned Scientists (UCS), and a bitterly fought struggle ensued between federal and industry officials insisting on the integrity of the technology and its economic blessings, and the growing grassroots movement that denied both. David Hunter and other donors were behind some of that activity, which hit a crescendo with the accident at Three Mile Island in March 1979. The near-disaster at the Pennsylvania nuclear plant occurred at about the same time President Jimmy Carter was retreating from his early emphasis on detente with Moscow and endorsing instead a passel of nuclear weapons—the multiheaded MX missile, the neutron bomb, the Pershing II, and cruise missiles intended to counter

Russian missiles in Europe. It all stimulated an atmosphere of all-things-nuclear going awry.

"Marianne Mott and I got together a large meeting in Maryland in the late '70s on nuclear power, with about forty funders and activists," David Hunter explains. Marianne Mott, Stewart Mott's sister and cobeneficiary of the General Motors fortune, played a role in two or three Mott philanthropies. "We were able to mobilize resources for work on nuclear energy *and* weapons. I always felt good about that meeting, bringing together constructive actors."

"One did get the sense that the anti-nuclear power folks were '60s activists in search of a cause," another donor of the period suggests. "They went from Vietnam to nuclear power to nuclear weapons and El Salvador, like a moveable feast of dissent."

The activist bridge between the two nuclear technologies was difficult to sustain. "I came from the part of the movement that worked on both," says Harriet Barlow, who in 1984 became director of the HKH Foundation. "It was a great mistake to divide these two. There was a natural link from nuclear weapons to environmentalism, but there were a few donors who said we can't 'pollute' it one way or the other." The two movements worked in parallel for a number of years all the same, crisscrossing again when the American factories that made weapons-grade uranium and plutonium became targets of the peace movement.

The most pressing dimension of the nuclear world in 1980, however, was the escalating tenseness of the U.S.–Soviet confrontation. While some donors like Bob Scrivner and Ping Ferry had long harbored fears about the possibility of nuclear war—Melinda Scrivner recalls her husband being deeply affected by a seminar on nuclear issues he took at Harvard, taught by Henry Kissinger—the hyperbolic rhetoric of the Reagan candidacy in 1980 drew others to the table. From the late 1960s to the mid-1970s, the United States and Soviet Union had one arms control triumph after another: the Nuclear Non-Proliferation Treaty (NPT), the Strategic Arms Limitation Treaty (SALT I), the Anti-Ballistic Missile (ABM) Treaty, the Vladivostok agreement, and the unratified SALT II. Suddenly, however, the long period of detente was crumbling. Soviet assertiveness in Africa, Central America, and the Middle East, new human rights challenges to Soviet repression, and a drumbeat of right-wing charges about Soviet cheating on the arms accords were corrosive. At the same time, the United States had suffered humiliations in Southeast Asia and most recently in Iran, where Shah Mohammad Reza Pahlavi was routed in January 1979. The reaction of Carter to the Soviets' bumptious behavior was to fall back on every presidents' favorite reflex: order up more nuclear weapons. Reagan raised the ante by claiming that Carter had been duped by the USSR, a charge that was all the more piercing when the Soviet Union invaded and occupied Afghanistan at the end of 1979. Clearly, a new and dangerous phase of the Cold War was afoot, and the nuclear threat was very much at the center of the commotion.

"We then tended to lump together the Pentagon, the CIA, the FBI, et cetera, into something we spoke of as the 'national security state,' and that was the real adversary," Leslie Dunbar recalls. "Bob Scrivner brought his Rockefellers into the campaign against nuclear weapons. A common goal could then be recognized, and Bob is due a lot of gratitude for his role in establishing it."

John Redick, then an executive at the W. Alton Jones Foundation in Charlottesville, Virginia, was a rarity among donors—someone with formal training in strategic studies. While he was not part of the "Hunter group," Redick reflects how the worries about nuclear weapons were becoming so widespread among donors in 1980. "All of a sudden the nuclear danger was in the headlines; it was finally being taken seriously," he says. "I thought there was some growing threat of accidental or unintentional war, and I was also concerned about regional situations, the Middle East, for example."

These two different, if related, motivations—actual concern about nuclear war and a broader critique of U.S. foreign policy—were readily forged together in the specter of a Reagan presidency and the signs of an authentic social movement in opposition. The Euromissiles issue—the deployment of U.S. nuclear weapons to counter Soviet missiles aimed at Western Europe—was arousing activist opposition in West Germany, the Netherlands, and Britain in particular, and by mid-1980 a full-blown social movement was visible. Not only was this surfacing (often with hostile coverage) in news media, but some prominent European peace activists had close ties to American donors, a key example being British historian and activist E. P. Thompson's friendship with Ping Ferry. The chance that profound opposition might emerge from the burgeoning movement in America, mainly then apparent in veteran peace groups like the Quakers' American Friends Service Committee, suddenly looked viable. Soon, more evidence was appearing. When a Massachusetts Institute of Technology graduate student named Randy Forsberg authored a call for something at first called a "nuclear moratorium," and then revamped to be known as a "nuclear freeze," it was quickly embraced by grassroots activists in western Massachusetts. They put the idea on local ballots, winning overwhelming support on the same day Reagan was elected. In this paradox the American social movement to end the Cold War reemerged in its most powerful, decisive stage.

INCHING TOWARD REBELLION

The approach Bob Scrivner took toward small but promising groups like the Physicians for Social Responsibility (PSR; its president, Helen Caldicott, was his muse on the nuclear peril) was illustrative of the early funding of disarmament campaigns. The first task was to alert the public to the mounting dangers of the superpowers' nuclear rivalry. Without an engaged public, little political power was available to the peaceniks. The Democratic Party was not amenable to their entreaties: Carter was doing everything possible to convert himself into a Cold Warrior. Ted Kennedy, who challenged Carter for the party's presidential nomination in 1980, had worked with the president's handlers to block a nuclear freeze proposal from the party platform. The congressional leadership looked even more cautious. The news media, as always, had its finger to the wind, but is always late to recognize social movements of any sort. The "people," that vague and oft-misused concept, constituted the only option for action. And the people knew little of the nuclear peril. "This was not a highly developed strategy," recalls Wade Greene in a typically modest assessment. "We put a lot of money behind Caldicott and PSR early, their town meetings around the country. We wanted to amplify the popular opposition and get the government to back away from the abyss."

"We didn't all come with the same objectives or techniques," Ed Lawrence of the Veatch Program recounts of the early years. "I looked for multiple groups for one problem area because you couldn't expect one group to do it all. We supported organizations with membership. They could generate public concern. If all you had was the Institute for Policy Studies making statements, nothing much was going to happen."

Meg Gage, a high school teacher and Clamshell activist who created a grassroots-oriented foundation, the Peace Development Fund, was at the center of the action in Amherst, Massachusetts, in the early 1980s. "What happened then was a back-and-forth between funders and activists. Peace funders 'came out of the closet' with this issue. The clarity of the nuclear threat made it easier for everyone to be involved. Bob Scrivner had the guts to fund PSR, then the Educators for Social Responsibility, and he brought a lot of others with him. Wade Greene is a saint, a heroic person. He was always there for the activists, for new ideas. Cora Weiss, too. These people did their homework, and became involved with the freeze groups and others in a way no other donors were, or have since."

The hands-on approach was new to philanthropy, at least in the arms-control field. Foundation officers may have read proposals for projects sent to them and occasionally met with the applicants. More conscientious types might have made "site visits" to see how their grantees were operating. But the deep, sustained involvement with an entire movement, present at the creation and building the structure of activism brick by brick, was highly unusual. Scrivner, Greene, Weiss, Hunter, Ferry, and others attended the meetings and conferences where the disarmament movement was being forged, lending the kind of financial and moral support that was indispensable to the activists. The larger political atmosphere, after all, was intimidating: Reagan, a cautious Congress, a standoffish policy elite, and a skeptical press were wary if not hostile to the freeze movement and allied groups, and it didn't take long for Reagan and his right-wing clique to accuse the freeze of being a tool of Soviet communism.

"After our electoral victory in 1980, the funders began to come in," recalls Randy Kehler, the national coordinator of the Nuclear Weapons Freeze Campaign. The Traprock Peace Center near Amherst spurred the nuclear referenda that were approved in fifty-nine of sixty-two communities in November 1980. "Sid Shapiro was an early supporter, the first grant to Traprock right after the '80 referenda. I recall several meetings with donors, strategy sessions. Wade Greene was an early and steady supporter. I remember Bob Allen standing up at a meeting of donors in 1981 and saying, 'If we're serious about nuclear disarmament, then we have to support the freeze. This has a much greater trajectory than anything we've ever seen, with much greater potential.' I was very grateful that Bob said that."

Not all the important early donors were part of the Hunter group. Alan Kay, a successful high-tech entrepreneur in Boston, was perhaps the first funder of the freeze. He met Forsberg when she spoke to his Unitarian congregation, and had her brief him weekly on nuclear disarmament perspectives. He accompanied her to a New York meeting at the 777 UN Plaza building that houses dozens of activist groups, at which she galvanized the gathering to embrace the nuclear freeze as a response to the likely Reagan buildup. He wrote a check for $10,000 to fund one of the ideas the New York meeting produced: a small conference in Washington to get the major public interest organizations to endorse the freeze. Kay remained an important backer of Forsberg and the freeze, and was a liaison to the business community as well.

Other early supporters of the freeze campaign included the Veatch Program and private donors like Jay Harris. Wade Greene estimates that his donors put "about a million" into the freeze between 1981 and 1984. Of course, the freeze campaign was a highly decentralized organization, a classic social movement, in fact, that had a loose confederation of local and state organizations that were "coordinated" by a national office in St. Louis, headed by Kehler. The national budget never exceeded $1.2 million. The locals had to raise funds themselves. "The freeze grew so quickly—maybe too quickly for its own good—that it was *the* context for funding," Meg Gage recalls. "We hadn't had a movement like that, and it really swept the country." Where PSR provided the shocking alerts about the medical consequences of nuclear war, the freeze infused disarmament activism with a democratic surge of undeniable power. In this, it presented a fundamental challenge to the system of nuclear decision making and to the rationales for nuclear doctrine, a far more radical critique than foundations were accustomed to funding. A number of organizations concerned about the arms race had been arguing for more moderate policies, in favor of the arms-control process that had reigned in the 1970s, but had never questioned the elite mode of policy formation nor the basic tenets of nuclear deterrence (*i.e.*, that the United States needed nuclear weapons to deter the use of such weapons by the USSR). The freeze excoriated both, and had remarkably broad-based popular backing for it. "We broke the 'trust us' idea of the nuclear elite. That notion was completely shattered by the freeze," contends Kehler. "It was also a great exercise in grassroots democracy, just getting so many people involved in this debate in so many ways." At its peak, there were two thousand freeze chapters across the country. For the whole of the disarmament movement, roughly 40 percent of all organizations were created between 1980 and 1983, three-fifths had fewer than five paid staff persons, and were mainly devoted to community education. This social movement was locally rooted, and its relative lack of experience would benefit from close attention from donors.

"Funders then were taking more initiative than usual," says Wade Greene. "I went to freeze meetings, the formative meetings with Caldicott and Forsberg and so on. We were in the trenches. We had close relationships. They usually don't want you there, and most of the time you shouldn't be there. But there was such a sense of *urgency*, this frightful menace, and things were happening so fast."

By 1982, a formidable challenge to official U.S. policy—and the way policy was being made—had been constructed. New professionally based organizations, women's groups, a smattering of unions, and hundreds of student clusters were joining in the upsurge led by the freeze campaign. A glance through grant lists and correspondence of the time conveys the breadth of the movement. There were thousands of church-based groups, led by Quakers and the Fellowship of Reconciliation, Vietnam-era groups like Clergy and Laity Concerned, and newer committees of Methodists, Presbyterians, Unitarians, and nearly every other Protestant denomination. The Conference of Catholic Bishops weighed in with denunciations of the nuclear madness, as did the National Council of Churches. Celebrity priests like the Berrigan brothers returned to public attention with their special brand of civil disobedience. The arrival of William Sloane Coffin at Riverside Church in Manhattan in 1978 was another symbol of the new religion of disarmament. Older groups like the Council for a Livable World and Women's League for Peace and Freedom revived and grew. The dissent-by-profession trend included collections of architects, lawyers, writers, nurses, athletes, engineers, teachers, economists, ranchers, soldiers, artists, homemakers, business executives, and musicians. Local organizers mounted campaigns to close military bases, convert defense manufacturers, ban missile silos from their open land, outlaw nuclear shipments, and close ports to nuclear-capable naval vessels. Towns and cities declared themselves "nuclear free zones" and paired with towns and cities in the Soviet Union. Delegations of legislators and mayors traveled to Moscow and Hiroshima and Washington to proselytize against the arms race. Dozens of advocacy think tanks sprang up all across the country to investigate the costs of Pentagon excess to their communities. Films, newsletters, curricula, and books proliferated. One in every four Americans had some connection to a peace group. Rarely has such a deep, pervasive, and multifaceted social movement grown and prospered like this outcry against the doctrine and deployments of nuclear weaponry.

The peace donors actually touched just a fraction of this panoply of protest. Of the national groups, about one-third of total budgets were supplied by foundations. Most of the movement was self-generated and voluntary, built on small donations of people in the communities they served. The Hunter group provided the seed money for virtually all of the national organizations, however, and underwrote the critical communities of scientists and other intellectuals who built the arguments and marshaled the evidence for disarmament. It was only too apparent, by 1982, that they had a tiger by the tail and didn't know whether to pull or let go.

HERDING CATS

"We came together to brainstorm," David Hunter remembers of the growing peace donor community, "and we did do a lot of talking together. We didn't come out with a major construction of a strategy. It was informal, only coordinated to a degree. It wasn't like, 'we're going to stop this by defeating this congressman.' It was more like, 'we're going to do so-and-so; why don't you come along?'"

"Hunter was good at making connections," says Ed Lawrence. "If we were interested in something, he would suggest an organization or person to see. We didn't all come with the same objectives or techniques. Each funder had his or her own preferences, something that got them excited. David seemed to be ahead of everyone else, he was there earlier, and he could identify the right people. But there was no joint funding. It wasn't that organized."

The Field Foundation was another with a track record in the disarmament area. Under Leslie Dunbar, it funded the Center for Defense Information—one of the first advocacy groups to document military waste—and some of the activist scientists like Frank von Hippel at Princeton, among others. Dick Boone, who had two separate tenures at the Field Foundation in the late 1970s and early 1980s, recalls a meeting in 1981: "A number of us came together—Wade, Ping, Cora, David, Carol Guyer, Dave Ramage—to try to figure out how to work together on a more continuous basis. I was on the way over with Rob Stein, and I said to him on the subway, 'Something has to come out of this, and I want you to run it.'"

The "something" was the Forum Institute, and Stein—a young lawyer who had worked on a Vietnam "boat people" project for Boone and Ramage—was indeed the person to head it up. The Forum was created to facilitate discussion among funders, and between grantees and funders. It produced reports, including an invaluable resource for the movement called *Search for Security*, which provided detailed data on funding trends and philosophy, as well as a compendium of foundations in the field. For the donors, Forum's utility was as a convenor and facilitator.

"There wasn't much strategy discussed during the meetings," Stein recalls. "Information sharing, talk about increasing the funding base, showcasing some groups and experts, that's mainly what we did. There was some backroom strategizing. I see some of it as strategic tools—shared information, or co-funding as leverage—like an investment banker does. It's as robust a role as a donor can perform.

"The strategy was to change the context in which policy makers had to respond. Five or six of this band of angels are responsible for driving a social change agenda that raised the issue's visibility and accessibility for the average person, and raised the comfort level for the Establishment fence-sitters. Remember, there was professional danger in the Reagan era in stepping out too far."

The danger may have accounted for the relatively slow entry of larger foundations into the disarmament picture. In 1982, seventy-four foundations active in the field provided $16.5 million in grants. (These were not all progressive donors, although most were, and the figures do not include Wade Greene's contributors or individuals like Alan Kay, Ping Ferry, or Jay Harris.) By 1984, the figure was $52 million, reflecting the arrival of the MacArthur Foundation and other giants. It was, to be sure, a still-tiny slice of American philanthropy: of the twenty-two thousand private foundations in the United States at that time, peace and international security funding comprised less than one percent of the total dollars given. But when one added in the impressive level of private donations—via direct mail, wealthy do-gooders, and the "tin cup"—the overall numbers were quite a bit higher, probably in the vicinity of $120 million or more. Greenpeace alone raised tens of millions annually in its door-to-door canvassing, and local groups took only one-sixth of their budgets from foundations.

So most freeze groups and allied church-based activists were rarely intimidated by the Reagan tactics. They already saw themselves as opponents of American policy. Many were veterans of the Vietnam War or civil rights movements, which were subjected to more vicious ostracism and threats. And financially, White House bullying may have slowed the pace of philanthropy, but most of the innovative groups partnered with the progressive donors and took comfort in each other's company. In the early 1980s, the first grant—the money for the risky project—for organization-building support most often came from the Hunter group, which extended its influence by being the first on the scene and sufficiently bold to get things done. "We would learn from each other," Bob Allen remembers, "and we would bolster each others' confidence. We all had boards to scrutinize our recommendations, and if we could say, 'well, these three funders are out front on this,' it would make it easier."

The small foundations, Stein says, had plentiful involvement from boards of trustees, as many of the donors were family-based entities, and this meant that formal collaboration and cofunding was difficult. "Relationships were somewhat delicate," David Hunter agrees. "I might have an idea and want to proceed and tell someone, FYI, I'm going to do this, and let him take from there. He would do the same towards me." So the Forum Institute gatherings in effect served the function of a classic peer group, where information became a vehicle of consensus-building. "If Bob Scrivner was going to fund something," a foundation executive at that time explains, "I would be attracted, because Bob was so well-informed, so serious and prudent, that I figured I just couldn't go wrong." The group in the early 1980s was self-selected progressive, more leftish than the movement itself, and that made broad agreement among donors more likely. That did not mean the agenda was overtly radical—"we have to sell peace like soap," Ping Ferry would say—but it did lend a certain coherence to action repertoires and expectations. So the "collaboration" was a forged sensibility of confronting Cold War institutions and rationales.

But it was the danger of nuclear war, the harrowing tension that was, in Bob Allen's phrase, "so real, so palpable, so gripping," that forged this sense of collective identity and collective (if haphazard) action. This unity of purpose was, paradoxically, reinforced and riven by the other major peace initiative of American activists and donors in the 1980s—the demand for an end to U.S. misbehavior in Latin America, South Africa, and the Middle East.

THE PARALLEL UNIVERSE
OF THE ANTI-INTERVENTIONISTS

Even before Reagan entered office, his designated secretary of state and UN representative, Alexander Haig and Jeane Kirkpatrick, were defending the El Salvadoran death squads that had murdered hundreds of dissidents in the previous months, including four American churchwomen in December 1980. Haig fired the U.S. ambassador to El Salvador, Robert White, a defender of human rights, within days of entering office, and forced out Anthony Pezzulo, the American envoy to Nicaragua. The Reagan team spoke of Nicaragua's Sandinistas as if they were the devil incarnate, a mortal communist challenge to the United States, and plotted their ouster. So from the first moments after Reagan's electoral victory, Central America was brought to the front burner as a place where the new, right-wing government would prove itself tough on communism. An anti-intervention movement, itself a mixture of Vietnam-era protestors, church people, and specialists on Latin America, rose to condemn the junta in El Salvador and the continuing horror of genocidal regimes in Guatemala, and to defend the prerogatives of the Sandinistas and other leftists to bring justice, however fitfully, to the beleaguered isthmus.

This movement, which had instant and largely reliable support from Democrats in Congress, operated in something like a universe paralleling the antinuclear movement. Many organizations such as the American Friends Service Committee, Mobilization for Survival, and Coalition for a New Foreign and Military Policy worked on both nuclear disarmament and intervention. The general outlook of both movements was similar: grassroots based, highly critical of U.S. policy and militarization, and scornful of the brutish anticommunism brandished by Reagan and conservative Democrats. But there were significant differences as well. The constituencies for each overlapped but were far from identical. "By 1984 there were two peace movements," explains Wayne Jaquith, an activist and Ploughshares Fund director in the late 1980s. "The anti-nuclear movement was white, middle class, professional, centrist, and east of the Mississippi. The anti-intervention movement was poor, significantly non-white, more radical, and less well-funded."

"The funders divided over Central America," recalls Harriet Barlow, whose HKH Foundation funded both. "Was the solidarity movement too radical? That may have been it. There were a few of the arms control types who did not want to be 'polluted' by Central America work. The funders could have bridged or negotiated between the two camps but instead chose sides. Very few chose Central America."

One obvious reason for the split was that the nuclear danger threatened everyone; Central America was a wholly different calculus. "It's hard to believe it was so contentious," says Meg Gage, also a donor to each cause at the Peace Development Fund. "The clarity of the nuclear question made it easier to grapple with. This was the Big One." Colin Greer, who worked with David Ramage at the New World Foundation and succeeded him in 1984, says of antinuclear philanthropy, "what seemed authentic was that funders for the first time were working on an issue in which they themselves could be a victim."

The freeze campaign was open to working with anti-interventionists, realizing that they were drawing from the same waters. "The 'freeze-as-floor approach' helped the groups avoid wrangles over when and how hard the campaign should hit intervention in El Salvador, American imperialism elsewhere, nuclear power, the conventional arms buildup," concluded a summary of a freeze campaign meeting at Blue Mountain Center, New York, in May 1982. "The consensus was that leaders of the national freeze must remain flexible and very attentive to how far grassroots support goes on these issues." The grassroots, especially the churches, remained active in both movements even if at the national level the two remained separate.

Unity eluded the activists protesting U.S. policy in Central America as well, clustered as they were into two camps: the "solidarity" groups, often encompassing grassroots activists, who expressed open support for the Sandinistas and the Farabundo Marti para la Liberacion Nacional (FMLN) rebels in El Salvador; and anti-interventionists, who simply opposed U.S. meddling but gave little open support to the leftists in the region. The differences were significant, with the solidarity movement often rejecting the "insider" deals cut by Washington-based groups working with members of Congress. But the protest around the country was essential to making the deals possible. The critical communities, often academics stirring in the Latin America Studies Association, fed both camps.

In Washington, the work of the anti-interventionists was remarkably effective with small financial resources at their disposal. "The strategy was based on the anti-Vietnam work originally funded by Stewart Mott," Bill Goodfellow recalls. A longtime Washington player in the nonprofit world, Goodfellow directs the Center for International Policy, which was in the thick of the Central American issue from the start. "Mott created the Coalition to Stop Funding the War in 1972, which was a new approach—convening different groups weekly to agree to work on at least one common piece of legislation. That's what we did on Central America. It was very effective." Because Democrats like Senator Christopher Dodd (D-Conn.) and Representative Joseph Moakley (D-Mass.) were readily willing to challenge Reagan policy in the region, the solidarity groups had direct access to congressional power and a relatively consensual platform. A number of the church-based groups, and Catholic groups in particular, became adept lobbyists. The goals were to deny the El Salvadoran junta military aid; likewise, to deny or condition aid to Guatemala and Honduras; and to end U.S. support for the *contras*, the right-wing army created in part by Reagan's CIA to overthrow the Sandinistas. There were a number of partial successes and as many setbacks in this campaign, and the movement was backed by a large and consistent majority of the American public.

A leading foundation supporting the solidarity campaigns was the Arca Foundation, the creation of an old Southern family of Smith Bagley; it was headed in this phase by Margery Tabankin, who was director of the Vista program during the Carter administration and later became a philanthropic force in Hollywood. The New York–based Funding Exchange, a hands-on "umbrella" for numerous small funds, was active with solidarity movements and the nuclear freezeniks as well. Others active in Central American work included the David Hunter philanthropies, the Youth Project, Agape and Vanguard foundations in San Francisco, and Bydale Foundation of New York, among many others. The MacArthur Foundation became active later in the 1980s.

The antiapartheid campaigns, many of the most vibrant of which were located on college campuses, had gathered steam in the 1970s and were becoming a worldwide force to end minority white rule in South Africa. Divestment campaigns were atop the agenda—encouraging a variety of major institutions, including universities, unions, and cities and states, to divest from their investment portfolios any companies doing business in South Africa. It was a resilient, durable campaign with a large measure of unassailable moral logic on its side, and, predictably, the Reagan administration stood against it. David Ramage brought the New World Foundation to the issue early on, joining the relatively small number of donors and organizations actively supporting antiapartheid activism; David Hunter and Cora Weiss were quite involved, as was the Norman Foundation in New York. This activism was yet another campaign tied closely to the churches, as was the anti-apartheid struggle within South Africa.

The antiapartheid movement fed and was fed by the meteoric growth of the human rights revolution. Its launching pad was Amnesty International, founded in 1961, and Helsinki Watch, later becoming Human Rights Watch, in the 1970s. The credo of "anti-intervention" typically referred to military intervention, but of course in South Africa, as in many other troubled venues of the world, the issue was not military intervention *per se*, but meddling of a pernicious kind, or malign neglect on the part of the U.S. government. In the Israeli-Palestinian issue, thousands of American Jews were mobilized on both sides of the "land-for-peace" equation. The contentious terrain of U.S. policy revolved around how strongly it tipped toward one position or another. But the issue played out often as a human rights matter. Jewish activists and organizations contributed significantly to the other peace movements of the 1980s, but their role in creating a peace lobby in this most important dimension of the Jewish Diaspora was crucial to progress in the Middle East by neutralizing the belligerence of prominent media celebrities like William Safire, Martin Peretz, and Abe Rosenthal. And the moral arguments of Peace Now USA or New Jewish Agenda hinged on human rights (including sovereignty) for Palestinians.

The human rights impulse gradually touched everything having to do with war and peace. The solidarity movements of Central America based virtually their entire case on human rights, broadly defined to include economic justice, which is probably one reason why the movement enjoyed such extraordinary levels of public support. Intervention was perhaps less the bugaboo than what *type* of intervention, since later ventures in the Balkans and Haiti seemed to earn high rates of approval from many of the same activists. And, just as intervention was a malleable concept, so too was the application of human rights: Disarmament activists were slow to condemn the Soviet Union for its blatant repression. By the early 1980s, however, the peace movements were reaching out to Eastern European dissidents in a systematic way, a gesture by Western Europeans that soon became a political tool in which both superpowers were castigated for their misbehavior on nuclear weapons *and* human rights. These links to and from Eastern Europe wedded movements for disarmament, human rights, and anti-imperialism.

As in Albert Einstein's theory of gravity, money will often flow toward impact, and one consequence of the persuasive power of human rights was that it attracted steadily increasing amounts of philanthropic dollars as its utility was repeatedly demonstrated. Even the nuclear weapons issue became more frequently defined as a question of human rights, the rights of the "unborn," to cite Jonathan Schell's assertive remark in *Fate of the Earth*, or the rights of neglected victims of radiation experiments, unsafe nuclear production plants, and Cold War militarization generally (including the casualties of U.S.–Soviet "proxy" wars). The possibility of war was pervasively spoken of as genocide. So human rights in the 1980s moved to the center of the movements for change, actually supplanting anti-interventionism, and this inevitably affected American philanthropy.

THE END OF THE BEGINNING

The gravitational force of the early to mid-1980s remained with the antinuclear movement, even as the freeze campaign declined after Walter Mondale's defeat in the 1984 election. As the movement grew, it attracted more donors, and the more donors it attracted, the more diluted the original group became. Some of the ringleaders began to drift away, or back to prior concerns, as bigger foundations stepped in with much larger sums of money. David Hunter's donors cut back in the nuclear weapons realm, as did the New World Foundation, while Bob Scrivner's death in 1984 drained some of the energy out of the original group.

Even before Scrivner's death, the shape of the citizens' campaigns to end the arms race had changed. Not only was the freeze campaign adrift, but the antinuclear movement was steadily becoming more professionalized, both in the sense of professions (doctors, lawyers, scientists, and educators) being central to the enterprise, and in the daily operations becoming more sophisticated, policy-oriented, and bureaucratic. Both of these trends were intentional on the part of many donors, Scrivner prominent among them. It had the effect of creating a more "credible" opposition in the eyes of elites, but it may have discouraged some at the grassroots who saw a new class of elites being created. While this discouragement was more apparent than real—an enormous amount and variety of protest persisted around the country throughout the decade—the perception was strong, for good or ill.

Two nodes of activity are emblematic of this trend—the "nuclear winter" study, and the opposition to "Star Wars," Reagan's plan for an antimissile shield. The latter was mounted by scientists, or science-based organizations, most important among them the UCS in Cambridge, with strong contributions from the Federation of American Scientists and some associations like the American Physical Society. I was involved with UCS in the days of Star Wars, and it was crystal clear that technical expertise was a necessary ingredient of opposition. This battle was over the feasibility of a system of strategic defense, and precious few had the keys to that kingdom of knowledge. The battle lines significantly excluded the grassroots, compared at least with the days of the freeze, because the Strategic Defense Initiative (SDI) was intuitively appealing (to make nuclear weapons "impotent and obsolete"), and the technical debate was dense and complex. Arguing effectively against SDI meant mastering this technical and doctrinal esoterica. So instead of simply expelling a primal cry against the nuclear madness, one had to be a physicist or engineer to make the case. In such circumstances, the critical community is more indispensable than ever, but the social movement is more constrained. Yet Reagan's Star Wars initiative was so important politically that donors recognized the fundamental need to stop it by investing in the professional groups.

The nuclear winter episode involved a simpler concept—the calculation that a nuclear war might dirty the atmosphere so much that a decades-long, winter-like climate change would ensue—but was still a matter of technical expertise. It was Bob Scrivner who picked up the notion, phrasing it as an environmental concern, and convening a small group of scientists, environmentalists, and donors to brainstorm in mid-1982. Among them was Carl Sagan, the celebrity-astronomer, who dramatically told the group at their second meeting that he was working with some California-based scientists who were building a computer model of this very thing—the environmental consequences of nuclear war. George Woodwell, the revered director of the Marine Biological Laboratory at Wood's Hole, did some back-of-the-envelope calculations as Sagan spoke, and then exclaimed, "Do you know what all of this would mean?" The virtual end of civilization. From there, a full-blown study was born, with a major conference and television "spacebridge" to Moscow, and a book by Sagan, *The Cold and the Dark*. The effect of the nuclear winter work was profound. By the time of the conference, it was another arrow in the quiver of the activists and intellectuals alike. Donors were front and center in the creation and fueling of the enterprise; after Scrivner's death, Bob Allen at the Kendall Foundation played the convening role to great effect. One consequence of the nuclear winter thesis, like the new emphasis on opposing Star Wars, was to move the center of gravity of the movement to the scientists, to the technical dimension of the critique. It was momentous for antinuclear politics and for the way the Cold War finally was resolved.

By mid-decade, the pioneers of the donor community had already helped launch a remarkable thing: the disarmament movement. The freeze campaign was wilting, but so many of its offshoots and similar species of opposition were thriving. The costs of the arms race and the obvious insanity of nuclear doctrines remained compelling focal points for American politics. The movement to end the nuclear threat had spurred a public demand that was simply undeniable. Most of that early group of donors continued to look for the way to "change the context," as Hunter puts it, "do things that would democratize the society and have some consequences for social and economic change." The movement they helped fuel to end the Cold War certainly fit that ambitious goal.

3

FUELING THE MOMENTUM

The Cold War was very much a going concern when Robert Winston Scrivner died in May 1984. Reagan was about to be reelected, this time by a large margin, and the issues of war and peace were central to the campaign. The Soviet leadership was doddering under the accumulated weight of its old, sclerotic leadership, then with Viktor Chernyenko in the first secretary's chair. Issues central to the "twilight struggle" were hotly debated: Star Wars, the MX, Pershing II, and cruise missiles for Europe, "no first use" of nuclear weapons, aid to the *contras*, the Soviet occupation of Afghanistan, the fate of Solidarity, and the bloody surrogate wars of southern Africa. The acrimony never seemed to ebb between those who regarded the Soviets as implacable foes hell-bent on world domination, and those who argued for peaceful coexistence and nuclear disarmament.

While it was apparent by mid-decade that the social movement to end the arms race had made an enormous, unprecedented impact on American society and politics, it was far from certain that this impact would carry the day. Both the grassroots activists and the critical intellectuals of the peace movement were neck deep in the debates of the times. The freeze campaign—which had managed, in its legislative strategy, to pass only a nonbinding resolution in the House, and in its electoral strategy to earn little—was limping toward a desultory merger with the National Committee for a Sane Nuclear Policy (SANE), the Coalition for a New Foreign and Military Policy was near collapse, and few other broad-based national organizations were thriving.

The news was not all bad. The new professional groups, and some that were simply revitalized, were doing quite well: Lawyer's Alliance for Nuclear Arms Control, Physicians for Social Responsibility, Union of Concerned Scientists (UCS), Educators for Social Responsibility, and so on and so on. The "critical communities" had jelled into formidable intellectual contenders—many of them the scientists so necessary for the technical critiques, but also historians, anthropologists, investigative journalists, and psychologists—and had seemed to capture, however tenuously, the favor of the major news media (which resulted from arduous, organized effort). Surveys showed increased public abhorrence at the thought of nuclear war. And, perhaps most important, a new leader finally made his way to the top Kremlin post when Mikhail Gorbachev became first secretary of the Communist Party in March 1985.

The second half of the decade would be dominated by Gorbachev's unique personality. But the American peace movement, even after the exhaustion of the "freeze moment," continued to press the public demand for disarmament, and was able to do so with more money, more knowledge, and more access than it ever had before.

WINSTON ENTERS

Within a year of Bob Scrivner's untimely death, the trustees he selected to govern the Winston Foundation for World Peace began to meet in New York. Few of the trustees knew each other, and apart from the one letter Bob left them, no instructions accompanied their mandate to work on the permanent prevention of nuclear war. So, at once, the foundation was forced to grapple with questions that frequently confront trustees of a new fund: What are we going to do?

The letter that Bob Scrivner wrote in March 1983 from his home in Connecticut was, as one would expect, insightful and straightforward. It did provide guidance, and the spirit was to aim high. "In the foundation field, there are foundations that are known as those that are at the leading edge of their particular subject matter area, and there are those that commonly follow along later" he wrote. "The Winston Foundation for World Peace should be thought of as a place where the most promising individuals or fledgling groups would naturally turn for their first or very early support." He provided five questions to ask about every potential grant—for example, whether it addressed a controversial subject—and he emphasized "charismatic leaders" as another criterion of support. But beyond that, and beyond what people knew of his own biases (activism over scholarship being one important standard), the work of the foundation was to be left up to the ten trustees.

One document circulated to the ten was Scrivner's program recommendations for the Rockefeller Family Fund (RFF), written in September 1981. The language of this twenty-six-page memo is cautious, reflecting, perhaps, his own sense of the limitations of that board. He had feared for his job, his widow recalls, because the direction he wanted to chart was so risky for the time, so contrary to the apparent, majority sentiment in the United States. The stated goal "could be simply to reduce the likelihood of nuclear war through arms control," he said after providing an overview of the arms race. He then mentioned seven specific goals, including maintaining an awareness of the consequences of nuclear war; limiting first-strike weapons; broadening the public debate about nuclear weapons; limiting arms spending; and nuclear nonproliferation. An emphasis on making the nuclear debate understandable to the public is evident, as is conveying the essential madness of the nuclear standoff. To that point, RFF had mainly supported the physicians' groups, and Scrivner wanted to continue down that track: "Because many of the issues are technical, it is envisaged that any substantial RFF program in the arms control field would include support of several public interest science groups specializing in these issues." Frank von Hippel's center at Princeton was mentioned in this regard, as were the Natural Resources Defense Council (NRDC) and the Council on Economic Priorities, whose directors became Winston Foundation trustees. He also cites a 1975 study by the National Academy of Sciences as a precursor to what became the "nuclear winter" thesis as an upcoming area of needed investigation.

Those he selected for the board, which is as important a decision as any benefactor can make, were a blend of people with experience in philanthropy and those who practiced the arts of peace advocacy, with two or three wise family friends included for good measure. They began to meet in New York in January 1985. For several months, they met with a range of experts—Richard Garwin and Pete Scoville at the first session, both weapons scientists; Ruth Adams, a physicist and head of the MacArthur Foundation program; and Freeman Dyson, another physicist. Interestingly, Ruth Adams advised that the area not getting attention now from foundations were the grassroots community groups.

By the autumn, a small conference was held at the Century Association that featured, among others, Morton Halperin, a prominent defense intellectual; John Pike, of the Federation of American Scientists; Tom Powers, a widely read author on nuclear matters; and Nick Dunlop, who headed Parliamentarians for Global Action, a group of legislators from around the world. They discussed the congressional responsibility for nuclear doctrine.

While the meetings were oriented to expertise, obviously, the sessions were helpful to orient members who were not knowledgeable about nuclear weapons issues. Many foundations throw their trustees into a decision-making cauldron with no preparation. The process Winston adopted, however, informed and unified the board, thereby letting a sense of direction emerge.

Among the results of the seven board meetings held in the first eight months was a statement of purpose, which noted a concentration on the political process. "Over the postwar decades, the political process in the main has failed to produce prudent decisions regarding the nuclear dilemma. A democracy needs an alert and active citizenry with access to accurate and sufficient information: it needs also governmental processes that are responsive to reasoned scientific and political analysis, that are effectively under civilian control and leadership, and that serve to build structures and relationships of world order and peace."

We decided to plunge into grant making as soon as I was settled in our new Boston office on Commonwealth Avenue, with Nancy Stockford coming with me from UCS. The board had done its preparation, and I saw no need to go through another period of thinking before we made grants. Bob Scrivner's old investment partner, Malcolm Wiener, was going to match our grants for the first six years—a model of private giving, in my view—so we were able to expend roughly $560,000 annually on grants in that period, not a huge amount, but in this field a significant dollar amount.

One of the first trips I took as executive director was to attend a donors meeting in New York. While the Forum Institute no longer shepherded this group, it still met once or twice a year. Of the original, most influential donors, Wade Greene, Ping Ferry, Anne Zill, Ed Lawrence, Carol Guyer, Cora Weiss, and Bob Allen were still actively engaged. David Hunter had cut back on his activities into a semiretirement. About thirty funders in all gathered on the top-floor conference room of 777 UN Plaza, with its spectacular view of the United Nations, on a sunny June morning in 1986. Most of the discussion is not memorable, except for two things, both of which were symbolic of where the peace movement stood at mid-decade.

First was a heartfelt plea by Meg Gage for donors to support a merger of the freeze campaign and SANE. Many saw this as a takeover of freeze groups by SANE, but the more charitable (and accurate) view was the necessity of merging an organization that still had considerable grassroots strength but no central nervous system, with a top-heavy Washington cadre that had no constituency. The fitful attempt to bring them together finally did succeed, with a name change in the early 1990s to Peace Action, which remains one of the few membership organizations dedicated to nuclear disarmament. A lot of energy was lost to the centrifugal forces of this spinning, flailing process of merger;

some blame the whole affair as a donor-demanded action, not needed and not wanted. But the end result was probably a net gain. The second was unexpected. Near the end of the meeting, John Adams and Tom Cochran of NRDC swept into the room and made a dramatic announcement: They had just come from the airport on their return from Moscow, where they had negotiated an agreement with the Soviet Academy of Sciences to create a seismic verification system in the USSR (and the United States). The room erupted in applause. It was indeed an astonishing achievement. A private, nonprofit organization—NRDC—had done what the U.S. government had refused to do and insisted was impossible to do: get the Soviets to agree to on-site verification of nuclear testing sites. Three seismic monitoring stations were set up near the Soviet test sites, and operated for several years, interrupted only by announced Soviet tests (in response to U.S. testing). The project not only spurred new rounds of debate about nuclear tests, but demonstrated how bilateral initiatives just below the official level, which would later be called "track two diplomacy," could be a regular instrument for peace making by nongovernmental organizations (NGOs). Within weeks of the agreement, the Soviet leader Mikhail Gorbachev announced an extension of the testing moratorium he implemented on the thirtieth anniversary of the U.S. bombing of Hiroshima, and days after that the U.S. Congress voted to impose a testing moratorium on the United States. Few doubted that the NRDC initiative bolstered both moves. The project, which cost NRDC $3.5 million over three years (the largest scientific endeavor in U.S.–Soviet history), displayed a level of technical and political sophistication inconceivable five years earlier. The project surely boosted the public's confidence in the wisdom and feasibility of a nuclear test ban.

Donors responded enthusiastically to NRDC's financial need to run the project. Bob Allen pledged $50,000 almost immediately, and several others of the original group were on board too, Wade Greene prominent among them. (Winston provided $50,000 in 1987.) What was more telling, however, were the new contributors to NRDC's breakthrough: $550,000 from the MacArthur Foundation, $200,000 from the Ford Foundation, and smaller grants from the Rockefeller Brothers Fund and Carnegie Corporation of New York. These large foundations were new, not to international affairs—Carnegie practically invented the field—but to the antinuclear movement. They would not easily have accepted the notion that they had joined this movement, but they had, by supporting not just NRDC but a number of other technically oriented arms-control projects. Since about 1984, these giants stepped in with some enormous contributions, and this fresh influx of money, coincidental with the decline of the freeze movement, exerted influence that was wholly commensurate with the grant sizes. It was, in effect, a midcourse "correction" in the strategy of changing U.S. nuclear policies.

THE MIDCOURSE CORRECTION

The programs of the new and large entries into peace funding stressed "strategic studies" at universities—Harvard's Kennedy School of Government was a favorite of Carnegie, Ford, and MacArthur—and the nonacademic analogue, the policy think tanks like the Brookings Institution and the Carnegie Endowment for International Peace. Some professional groups gained favor, as did smaller, "advocacy" think tanks (or "opinion tanks" as one donor sardonically called them), which were undertaking serious analysis of nuclear weapons policy. Given the animus of the Reagan administration to anything smacking of arms reductions, these grants constituted support for critical communities that fed, however unintentionally, the still-verdant grassroots active around the nation.

The decision by Carnegie and MacArthur to enter the field with such force derived, as is so often the case in foundations, from the personalities at the helm. The John D. and Catherine T. MacArthur Foundation was endowed by a man who apparently cared little about what his legacy would produce. By the early 1980s, the foundation was ready to give away money but had no clear sense of purpose. Two board members, Jerome Wiesner, the former president of Massachusetts Institute of Technology (MIT) and President John F. Kennedy's science adviser, and Murray Gell-Mann, a prominent physicist, recruited Ruth Adams from her editor's chair at the *Bulletin of the Atomic Scientists* to help them formulate the program. "We wanted to support a new generation of people to look at this nuclear issue," she recalls. "We also looked at the public interest community, and hoped to put them in touch with networks of common interest. And the Soviet Union: there was a sense something was going to happen. We didn't know what it was, but war was not out of the question. So we presented a program to the board in December 1984 that included education, research, international action, and public interest groups." In its early years, some $25–30 million annually would be dedicated to the program Adams was to head—an enormous sum.

Adams, Wiesner, and Gell-Man were influenced by an April 1984 memo authored by McGeorge Bundy, who had been national security adviser to Kennedy and Lyndon B. Johnson, and then served as president of the Ford Foundation from 1967 to 1979. The memo was also written for Carnegie and its new president, David

Hamburg. Bundy drafted the memo with the aid of a number of prominent arms-control mavens: Graham Allison at the Kennedy School, Sidney Drell at Stanford University, George Rathjens at MIT, and John Steinbruner at Brookings among them. The twenty-six-page document strongly recommended several areas for funding: "the commanding need for a deeper understanding of behavior within and between the United States and the Soviet Union," and a need "for deep and serious efforts to understand the specific problems posed by the nuclear arsenals of the superpowers." One might have been surprised, in the middle of the 1980s, by the supposition that the problems of the nuclear danger were significantly unknown, but that was this group's recommendation, a group of individuals who were of course engaged in precisely these two arenas of research. (Bundy submitted a separate memo from himself alone recommending large grants to the institutions of the individuals on his team, and those grants were made, totaling $4 million from MacArthur.) The group, noting its own interest, asserted that "we know of no important research center in this field that is currently exempt from severe limitations on its resources which restrict the effectiveness of its work." The memo went on to argue for ample, multiyear support for a small number of research centers, scholars, and graduate students. It urged the two foundations to support "regular access to independent and technically authoritative comment on those parts of emerging issues which are amenable to nonpolitical and solidly based technical analysis." As to the large field of advocacy groups (such as the Federation of American Scientists or the Arms Control Association), the Bundy team says "we have made no detailed study of them. Such a study might well show that one or more of these organizations has a superior record in the encouragement of political awareness of particular issues affecting nuclear danger, and many of us, though not all, are inclined to believe that a foundation prepared to support the staff work necessary for discriminating choices could find excellent targets of opportunity in this group." Nothing like a social movement was mentioned.

What is striking about the Bundy memo, which had direct influence with the donors and was also representative of a prevailing spirit among the large foundations, is the absence of any strategy of how to change policy. The implicit assumption—tacit because it didn't need to be stated by this group or likely readers—was that decisions about nuclear policy are made by elites, whether political or bureaucratic elites, and better, smarter information (from the prestigious institutes) is the route to affecting these decision makers. So support for elite institutions and technically oriented ("nonpolitical") work constituted the core of the recommendations. The memo was entitled, "To Make a Difference."

To her credit, Ruth Adams went well beyond Bundy's ivy-covered memo and funded a number of more assertive projects—in 1986–87, for example, the foundation supported broad public education via the PBS television series, "The Nuclear Age"; peace studies programs; professional groups like the Lawyer's Alliance for Nuclear Arms Control; the Center on Budget and Policy Priorities to examine defense spending; *Nuclear Times*, the movement's magazine; and think tanks like the Institute for Policy Studies, the National Security Archive, and Center for War, Peace & the News Media. The grants to individuals were even edgier: John Cavanaugh and Robin Broad, on emerging trade issues; William Arkin, the Greenpeace nuclear gadfly; Virginia Gamba, on the arms trade; and Lars Schoultz, an expert on human rights in Latin America, among others, encompassing a broad swath of topics by people widely identified as progressive thinkers. While supporting the academics and interdisciplinary studies, Adams was also raising the dollar level precipitously for the critical communities.

The Carnegie Corporation apparently tracked Bundy's thinking more closely. In 1984, the fund, which spent only $15,000 two years earlier in this field, made grants of more than $6 million by supporting Harvard (more than $1 million); American Academy of Arts & Sciences, MIT (more than $1 million); the Aspen Institute, Columbia University; and the Brookings Institution, all for "Avoiding Nuclear War" (the foundation's program name) or to examine Soviet behavior. Carnegie became particularly wedded to problems of nuclear management—command and control, accidental war, and the like—which, inevitably, were mainly technical in nature. Ford was also supporting academic institutions in this field, but had an enormous program in human rights as well, which provided a seed bed for future trends in issues of war and peace. Uniquely, at that time, Ford had field offices around the world, and this too provided a wholly different look to their grant profile.

Others of the giants lumbered into the field. The Rockefeller Brothers Fund (RBF) developed a program in 1982–83, partly with the informal guidance of Bob Scrivner, which emphasized nuclear nonproliferation, consequences of nuclear war (as in the nuclear winter thesis), and "new paths" to arms control, though the latter category was dropped in the late 1980s. "Bob Scrivner had told me that there were three stages of a strategy," says Hilary Palmer, the RBF program head in the 1980s. "One, raise public awareness. Two, figure out what to do. Three, try to do it. We did number two—analysis. We never engaged the trustees in discussions of social change, because RBF was already doing analysis. Our discussions were more along the line of 'this guy is smart and wants to do this. . . .' There wasn't a whole lot of philosophy behind it, although we were drawn to people who had solutions. And MacArthur and Carnegie were coming in with some big money, and that affected some of my thinking." RBF, like the other large funds, tended to see itself as promoting informed debate, saw the need for more research, and aimed to support arms control that would stabilize nuclear deterrence. Prophetically, Palmer argued in a memo to her board in 1984 that proliferation needed more emphasis because no one else was doing it. "Ironically, horizontal proliferation is getting so little attention and funding because it does not seem like today's problem, but more like tomorrow's." By funding horizontal proliferation, she wrote, RBF "would be acting with foresight to help stave off future dangers rather than simply reacting to the now increasingly widely perceived present dangers relating to nuclear weapons." RBF was very much in the stream of supporting the analytical community—it hadn't the slightest taste for popular movements—but its emphasis on policy (in contrast to academic study) and its clarity of purpose made it an unusually effective player over the ensuing decade.

The debate within funding circles and the arms-control community about the specific approach to change—thinkers versus doers, or academics versus grassroots activists—was ongoing and at times heated. The chasm between some defense intellectuals and activists often appeared broad and deep. A series of meetings between Kennedy School honchos (Joe Nye, Al Carnesale, and Graham Allison) and the publisher of *Nuclear Times*, Richard Healey, and occasionally other activists was one attempt to bridge the gap. "The idea, which was funded by Fritz Mosher at Carnegie, was to see if there were things they were doing that could help the peace movement, and to see if some of our insights and concerns might inform them," Healey recalls. "But they weren't interested. We were like an alien species."

But there were highly skilled intellectuals who were ready and willing to feed the activist side: Frank von Hippel at Princeton, Jerry Wiesner, Victor Weisskopf, and Henry Kendall at MIT, Richard Garwin at IBM, Herb Abrams at Harvard Medical School, Robert Jay Lifton at Yale University, among many others. The fact that so many of these were scientists speaks volumes, too, about their willingness to overcome their social inhibitions to cooperate with the great unwashed of the grassroots. "MacArthur would say 'we support an active approach,' and then ask, 'what is the policy work to back this up?'" observes Harriet Barlow, the director of the HKH Foundation. "By comparison, when funders say 'we *only* talk to policy people,' then they can't make a strategy that works. You must have all kinds in the room."

What became apparent was that certain circles of defense intellectuals were important mainly because their profile had been raised by large foundation grants. This feature is one of the distorting qualities of large-scale philanthropy, namely, the creation of an undeserving force that then demands attention from others. A staggering amount of money went to university centers where the primary purpose was the maintenance of the status quo, perhaps a better managed status quo, but the status quo all the same.

The more productive, not to say the more normatively appealing, strategy was to fund intellectuals that did see themselves as agents of change, people who embraced the possibility of significant nuclear weapons cuts and improved U.S.–Soviet relations. This strategy was one of change that was increasingly if awkwardly embraced by foundations in the mid to late 1980s. Among the results of this strategy was a higher level of technical competence within the public interest groups—a physicist like Tom Cochran at NRDC, for example, or a space-weapons expert like John Pike at the Federation of American Scientists, or a nuclear know-it-all like William Arkin at Greenpeace. There were public interest think tanks created specifically to serve the purpose of providing expertise, most notably Randy Forsberg's Institute for Defense and Disarmament Studies. The Wiesners, Garwins, and Weisskopfs would often then work through them.

The trend toward professionalization was timely, as it happened, because the debates about the nuclear danger by about 1986 were mainly riveted on the details. The public was on-board for detente and arms cuts. The government scientists from Los Alamos or Livermore could no longer have the field to themselves; instead, they had to compete with highly skilled analysts backed by public relations staffs and large memberships.

By 1987, the chance of deep cuts was in fact a very real possibility, given the overtures of Gorbachev and the results of the Reykjavik summit, where the two leaders nearly cut a deal for the elimination of all nuclear weapons. Such an atmosphere should have emboldened all foundations, and some responded to the stimuli.

CASHING IN

Our initial strategy for change was mindful of the role of the professionals in the push for disarmament. I came from UCS, where I had argued for the same, high level of skills that UCS's nuclear power program had long enjoyed. Two members of the Winston board, Alice Tepper Marlin of the Council on Economic Priorities and John Adams of NRDC, were part of the professionalization trend, and Bob Allen of the Kendall Foundation was one of its supporters. This strategy was to be a prominent theme of Winston Foundation grant making: increasing the sophistication and credibility of the peace movement, while pushing the envelope conceptually, and maintaining a healthy respect for the role of local activism.

These sentiments translated into support for several of the best critical thinkers—Randy Forsberg, the World Policy Institute, and the Environmental Policy Institute among them. The grassroots were backed with support for the merger of SANE and the freeze campaign, campus activism, and twenty local groups like Nebraskans for Peace and the Hanford Education Action League. Several media projects gained favor, including *Nuclear Times*, radio "magazine" shows, and an innovative program to educate American correspondents in Moscow, run by the Center for War, Peace, and the News Media. We promoted a number of unofficial diplomacy efforts through U.S.–Soviet exchanges at varying levels that engaged everything from policy brainstorming to film. And we invested in a few experiments, such as a global verification scheme, which meant to break through some of the barriers blocking nuclear weapons cuts.

At best, we strove for a combination of projects that could advance the momentum for disarmament. A good example was stirred by a talk I heard at the 1986 meeting of the National Network of Grantmakers by Robert Alvarez of the Environmental Policy Institute. Alvarez, in his methodical but quietly impassioned way, described the alarming conditions in the nation's nuclear weapons production complex, the seventeen facilities that produce plutonium and highly enriched uranium, and fabricate nuclear explosives. This complex, Alvarez patiently explained, was hazardous to the workers and surrounding communities, could not account for all the plutonium it made, and created constituencies that would lobby against arms reduction treaties. In an especially striking way, Alvarez asserted that the complex's radioactive effects were "like a slow-motion nuclear war" against the American people. We quickly supported Alvarez's program of analysis and networking, and funded four of the local groups working in the afflicted communities. The strategy was aimed to spur the local outcry against those facilities and then match that protest with knowledgeable policy work on Capitol Hill. (While not wholly successful, a number of remedial measures were forced on the overseer, the Department of Energy, and a few of the plants were closed.)

The weapons-complex campaigns were part of a broader strategy to extend the stigmatization of all things nuclear beyond the U.S.–Soviet arms race. The nuclear danger was here, in our backyard. It was also being exported: hence, grants to Gary Milhollin and his remarkable research and advocacy on nuclear-related exports. It was also incurring staggering financial costs: hence, grants to the Council on Economic Priorities to look into the real costs of Star Wars. In a 1988 review of our first two years of grant making, I described this strategy to the Winston board. Change comes from the "top," such as policy makers in Washington; from "below," such as local action groups, politicians, and institutions; and from outside influences, such as world events, and international campaigns. "Virtually every policy change will exhibit these three influences in varying quantities," I wrote then. "We should also seek to reform or strengthen the process of change, however ... So, for instance, we support ways to empower local activists because local activism in the United States is pro-disarmament; we also believe the decision-making process should be opened up to more public scrutiny and influence." Part of the task, I concluded, was not only to commit to a strategy of change, but to find the innovators who could challenge the orthodoxies of the Cold War, whether through conceptual work (particularly "common security" and "nonoffensive defense"), new channels of influence (mainly through the news media), or new ways to empower disarmament advocates (through unofficial diplomacy, giving voice to dissident officials, or promoting electoral tactics).

Of course, we were not doing this by ourselves. While we were the first to fund several initiatives, many of the activist-oriented funders had similar grant-making profiles, among them the Wade Greene donors, Ploughshares Fund, Rubin Foundation, Kendall Foundation, and the Veatch Program—significantly, nearly all from the original 1980–81 group. The opposition to Reagan's Central American policies was in full flight as well. There was, we found in the first two years of funding, an enormous reservoir of energy and inventiveness at the grassroots. The decline of the freeze and its torturous merger with SANE is often mentioned as evidence of an exhaustion of local, popular will and commotion, but that was not the case. There was a "shakeout," to be sure, but the durability of projects and their variety was the bigger story, a story built by the growth and sudden emergence of groups of locally elected officials, a new genus of campus organizing and the full flowering of peace education, the sister-city networks, nuclear-free zone campaigns, women's initiatives, the weapons-complex work and other environmental links, and so on. The rise of the professional organizations itself was very much linked to local activism: Most of those organizations had memberships, even a local-chapter structure, from which they derived their strength. Four of them formed a Professionals' Coalition for Nuclear Arms Control, headed by David Cohen, one of the savviest strategists in Washington, to harness the local lobbying power of the scientists, doctors, lawyers, and educators.

The activist donors' "midcourse correction" had much to do with this continuous appearance of new initiatives and constituencies. The professionals' groups, while aided directly or indirectly by the entry of the giant philanthropies, earned their most important support from these smaller donors or from their own memberships.

The donors, large and small, continued to gather once or twice a year in large meetings, often to hear from the practitioners, just as we did on that sunny June day when John Adams made his dramatic entrance with news of NRDC's seismic monitoring initiative. But the relations between donors were not as tight as they were at the beginning of the 1980s. The Forum Institute was no longer retained to coordinate, and meetings were at the mercy of whoever decided it was time to get together. More often, foundation officers acted alone, or through informal networks of consultation. In my experience, the lack of more intentional collaboration was a surprise and a disappointment. Occasionally one sees an article in *The Nation* or some other opinion journal that presumes cabal-like webs in funder relations, which is a wholly laughable conjecture. The opposite is closer to the truth: Donors tend to be far too isolated, working by themselves with other staff and board members and overly influenced by a few persuasive grantees. One must make an effort to get out, read widely, and talk with everyone. If a funding strategy has been consciously formulated, then such exposure will only enhance the funding portfolio. But as a small donor, effectiveness ultimately must be derived in part from collaboration.

Such cooperation was haphazard, but still packed a punch in the second half of the 1980s because the donors were essentially on the same page strategically. The combined impact of the groups we all funded was to keep the popular pressure on the administration to deal on arms reductions, to cobble together coalitions on Capitol Hill to impose restraints on the arms race, and to open new, problem-solving ventures with Soviet counterparts. By 1988, with the first major breakthrough in arms reductions—the Intermediate Nuclear Forces (INF) Treaty that removed all such missiles from Europe—it was obvious that the efforts were paying off. We were beginning to cash in on all the investments made in the previous decade.

4

HOW WE ENDED THE COLD WAR

Any candid assessment of peace philanthropy's impact in the 1980s turns on the question of why the Cold War ended. Few donors included this as an aspiration, but its main constituents—nuclear arms cuts and U.S.–USSR detente—were explicit goals. The human rights movement and the European peace movement also saw expanding political freedoms for Eastern Europe as a key objective. So the end of the Cold War, which effectively came to a close with the tearing down of the Berlin Wall in November 1989, and officially concluded with the demise of the Soviet state twenty-three months later, fulfilled many of the hopes and dreams of peace activists, given that the rationale for nuclear readiness was the U.S.–USSR rivalry. But did the peace activists have much to do with it?

The answer, of course, is complex. Typically, one responds according to ideological predisposition. The hyperbolic debates of the 1980s over nuclear weapons, the *contras*, apartheid, and other such issues, coupled with the swiftness with which communism receded, made cool assessments of this question difficult until recently. Outcomes also seemed mixed: A "victory" for Reagan's policy in Afghanistan seemed apparent in 1988, but much less so in the late 1990s as the more durable (and grisly) consequences of arming the *mujaheddin* became apparent. For solidarity movements, a victory for antiapartheid activists in South Africa in 1989 was perhaps tempered by more ambiguous results in Central America in the early 1990s. Even what appeared to be an unstoppable momentum for nuclear disarmament in 1988–92 has flagged.

But the Cold War did end, and many of its worst features ended with it—the nuclear arms race and the threat of intentional nuclear war between the superpowers, Soviet repression, surrogate wars, and the division of Europe. How and why this forty-year standoff was concluded are fateful questions. It is said that victors never learn lessons.

As the apparent winners, the West needs to carefully examine this most momentous competition of the twentieth century to learn the correct lessons about avoiding war and ensuring peace. Among those students should be the philanthropic community, within which many people helped set in motion the forces that brought this most dangerous confrontation to a conclusion.

THREE VIEWS ON THE DEATH OF THE COLD WAR

Three main interpretations of the Cold War's demise are prominent, not surprisingly reflecting the right, center, and left of American politics.

From the tearing down of the Berlin Wall, the right wing immediately claimed a resounding victory for Reagan's military buildup and tough talk. Their reasoning pivots on the intimidating qualities of the U.S. arsenal (especially Star Wars), NATO's stalwart rejoinder to the Soviet SS-20s with Euromissiles, and the Reagan Doctrine of battling communist regimes in southern Africa, Central America, and, most decisively, Afghanistan. The rapid expansion of U.S. defense spending, it is argued, also threatened Moscow with bankruptcy. Given the dismal prospects of trying to keep up with the American technological juggernaut and protect its puppet regimes, the Politburo sued for peace by electing Gorbachev. Some Reaganites even assert that this was their intention all along, to crush the Soviet Union and win the Cold War.

Centrists in the Democratic Party saw things differently. They argued that the forty-year effort to check and reverse Soviet influence was a bipartisan endeavor. The core of America's strategy—the policy of containment—was forged in the late 1940s by Harry S. Truman's advisers, such as George Kennan, Paul Nitze, and others, and carried out with persevering fidelity. Truman, Kennedy, and Johnson played indispensable roles in standing up to the USSR, a Democratic Congress authorized the policy and the money, and even the much-maligned Jimmy Carter ordered up the neutron bomb, MX missile, Euromissiles, and anticommunist actions in the Third World. The European alliance, which included many democratic-socialist governments over the years, was vital to the outcome as well. Diplomacy played a major role, as did foreign aid, trade, the communications revolution, and other factors. Gorbachev came to be regarded as a kind of improvising reformer who saw the Soviet Union as dysfunctional, but whose *perestroika* was unworkable and whose *glasnost* careened out of control. Reagan just happened to be there at the end.

Yet a third view saw the Cold War as a logical, and reprehensible, outgrowth of an American political system seemingly dependent on military spending for prosperity, constantly in need of an enemy, determined to maintain class and race privileges for the few, and willing to put the whole world at risk for its perfervid anticommunism. This perspective, which often (though not often enough) imputed similar qualities to the Soviet Union, was the cornerstone of the New Left that so effectively challenged U.S. policy in Southeast Asia in the 1960s and early 1970s. By the early 1980s, this perspective was invigorated by a mass movement that was a hybrid of many gradations of political sentiments. Its engine was political participation, and, naturally enough, the demise of the Cold War is seen mainly as a result of citizen activism. This activism included efforts to stop and reverse the arms race, counteract the power of the military-industrial complex, condemn the U.S. government's comfort with apartheid, and overturn the U.S. imperialism conspicuous in Central America and the Caribbean. The tonic for each of these American maladies was public education, mobilization, and pressure. In this vision it was far more limited than that of the New Left, but its central emphasis on public participation (very much a legacy of the Port Huron Statement) served as both a strategy and explanation for how that action succeeded.

Central to the peace movement's reckoning, however, is the indispensable role of Gorbachev. It was his recognition of the recklessness of Cold War policies on both sides that brought an end to the rivalry. The American activists did much to constrain the excesses of the Reagan era and build a public demand for arms reduction and detente. They formed the campaigns to defund the *contras*, end apartheid in South Africa, and promote human rights throughout the vast expanse of the world where the U.S. government was silent. These actions not only had profound consequences for U.S. policy, but transformed the context of American politics and enabled Gorbachev's reforms to succeed in the United States. The American public was ready and willing to accept his entreaties, and were ready sooner than virtually all political and opinion leaders. A parallel phenomenon was unfolding in Europe, which had the further dimension of cultivating civil society in Eastern Europe. This activism on two continents created pressure on the Atlantic Alliance to bargain ambitiously, and in good faith, with Gorbachev, while simultaneously holding Gorbachev to the substance of his propaganda.

In these three interpretations of why the Cold War ended, it is notable that the last Soviet leader is seen by all three claimants as the pivotal figure. But the hows and whys of his actions vary widely in interpretation: the right thinks Reagan forced him to disarm, the center sees him as a good-willed if somewhat unintentional partner in defusing the rivalry, and the left regards him as a revolutionary avatar of peace focused on ending the Cold War. His motives and actions, and his impact in Western Europe and the United States, are in effect the keys to unlock this mystery.

THE REAGAN VICTORY AND CONTAINMENT'S TRIUMPH

The right wing's declaration of victory rests mainly on its belief in the power of bluster. The Soviets folded because Reagan intimidated them by brandishing an array of sharp tools: nuclear weapons, force projection, anticommunist crusades in Central America, southern Africa, and Afghanistan, and a grandiloquent campaign for personal freedom in the Soviet empire. No doubt these tactics did present a formidable escalation of long-standing American tactics. The question is whether they were, as a whole, sufficient to lead Gorbachev to surrender.

Some of these claims can quickly be discarded. The call for liberty was hardly unique to Reagan; it had been a standard rhetorical device for forty years. The Helsinki accords of 1975, which established a human rights framework for all of Europe, had been denounced by the right wing. Jimmy Carter, the first president to make human rights a core goal of U.S. foreign policy, was condemned by conservatives for placing rights above other national interests. The advent of human rights as a viable political issue was itself a creation of civil society: Amnesty International, founded in 1961, and Human Rights Watch, created ten years later, were the leaders in adding rights to the global agenda, and they were fastidiously balanced in their criticisms of repression. Years of effort to forge links to Eastern European dissidents had been pursued by a number of nongovernmental actors, many of them in the European peace movement. The right wing, which was incensed at the human rights program for years, borrowed freely from it to turn up the heat on the USSR. But the Reagan administration was flagrantly hypocritical about rights. Not only could it tolerate and even embrace regimes that were among the worst offenders—South Africa, Turkey, El Salvador, Argentina, Chile, and so on—but it created and funded movements in the name of fighting communism that committed numerous atrocities. The bombast about communist oppression rang hollow when one heard comments, for example, from Secretary of State Alexander Haig that the Maryknoll nuns murdered in El Salvador by the U.S.–backed military were revolutionaries who essentially deserved their fate.

The Reagan Doctrine had the same flavor. The United States relied on a strategy of supplying weapons large and small to a variety of guerrillas and allies for thirty years, and its record of success was meager at best. The military support for the Shah of Iran, for example, imploded in the Islamic Revolution. In response to that debacle, President Reagan provided covert financial, intelligence, and equipment aid to Saddam Hussein, with disastrous consequences. Arming other friendly, scarcely democratic regimes, from Indonesia to El Salvador, produced similarly sordid results. That was the "Nixon Doctrine."

The Reagan Doctrine added a new dimension: supplying guerrillas in Angola, Nicaragua, and Afghanistan to battle supposedly Marxist regimes. There is little doubt that the Afghan fighters, lavishly supplied by the CIA, helped to convince the Soviets to leave Afghanistan, and the CIA–backed *contras* destabilized Nicaragua enough to tip an election against the Sandinistas. The civil wars in Angola, which took a million lives, were negotiated to a settlement, although the Reagan-backed insurgents refused to cooperate and continued to wreak havoc in the country.

The costs of those "victories" were not only bloody (Afghanistan now a wasteland, ruled by the ruthless, anti-American Taliban, a descendant of the *mujaheddin*, and Nicaragua an impoverished shell), but were hardly decisive in the undoing of Soviet communism. Neither Angola nor Nicaragua was consequential to the Soviets. Afghanistan was important, of course, and the calamitous occupation begun in 1980 did resonate through Soviet society. From an early period in that debacle, however, Soviet leaders—including Leonid Brezhnev as early as the spring of 1980—sought a way out; it was obvious in Moscow that the USSR was overextended. Gorbachev and his contemporaries also recalled the fateful and, in their view, shameful Soviet interventions in Hungary in 1956 and Czechoslovakia in 1968. The bulk of aid to the *mujaheddin* came in the late 1980s, most prominently after March 1986, a year after Gorbachev came to power with the intention of withdrawing Soviet troops from Afghanistan. That it took three more years to act on that intention reflects the same sort of face-saving difficulty that ensnared the United States in Vietnam. But it is a stretch to claim that the counterinsurgency in Afghanistan was a decisive blow to the Soviet Union's very existence.

The *contra* war was significant only because of its high profile in the United States. Gorbachev kept up large infusions of aid into Nicaragua right to the end of Reagan's presidency, and stopped only when the U.S. tactic shifted from counterinsurgency to diplomacy. The Soviets even bargained for free elections in 1990 and declined to provide aid to the Sandinistas to help them win the elections because, in the words of one senior Soviet official, "We didn't think it was a good investment."[1] So the *contra* war did not bully Moscow; quite the opposite. Gorbachev's willingness to jettison Daniel Ortega in 1990 also shows what a low priority Central America was for the Soviets. Only Cuba, with its exceptional symbolic importance, came close to the Reagan depictions of the region being a vital battleground between the superpowers.

The enormous investments the Reagan team made in the region to topple Fidel Castro and Ortega and decisively defeat the leftist rebels in El Salvador, reflected their own ideological need to confront communism, but the crusade never resonated with the American public. (Reagan went so far as to call the *contras* the "moral equal of our Founding Fathers.") This failure to persuade was all the more remarkable given the low ratings for Castro and the Sandinistas. Unlike, say, South Africa, where apartheid was viewed as an abomination that should not be accommodated, Americans had no taste for Marxist revolutionaries no matter how despicable their enemies. Yet despite the colossal effort that Reagan and his lieutenants put into the actual zones of conflict—the results of which were devastating for Central America, of course—and into the zones of debate in the United States, the American people never bought in.[2] Opposition to aid for the *contras*, for example, was never less than 62 percent during the 1980s, and a growing majority also disdained Reagan's overall policies in Central America.

The Reagan Doctrine faced similar rejection in southern Africa. While the public was scarcely aware of the extent of U.S. mischief, the policy of "constructive engagement" with Pretoria was never embraced by the American public. Reagan's own State Department was arguing for a more liberal policy—one senior official even stated in 1984 that "Southern Africa is well outside the Soviet Union's zone of primary interest, indeed of secondary interest"—while the president was inveighing against black nationalists as communist terrorists and, with Margaret Thatcher, finding ways to support the apartheid government. This cornerstone policy was renounced by the Republican Senate in August 1986 when it approved a tough sanctions bill by a vote of 84–14.[3]

One key survey found that military aid to counterinsurgents in all these venues, including Afghanistan, was very unpopular. In 1986, when Reaganites could argue that the policy was showing some results, the American public gave it only 24 percent approval. Nearly a majority disapproved outright, while 30 percent said they would agree to economic aid only for the insurgents.[4] This after years of anticommunist drumbeating and before Gorbachev had made an impression on the Western mind. This shortage of public favor was hardly the footing for a campaign intended to intimidate Moscow.

Probably the dominant perception today about the Cold War's unraveling is based on the idea of exhaustion: The Soviets, facing bankruptcy, opted for an arms-reduction strategy to defuse the rivalry and enable them to invest in their chronically ailing economy. This view is particularly tempting because it fulfills one of the treasured shibboleths of the Cold War—capitalist plenitude versus socialist deprivation—and it heroically justifies the immense costs of the contest. And there is enough truth to this idea to lend it an air of invincibility as *the* explanation. Gorbachev certainly regarded the U.S.–USSR competition as irrationally enervating (an opinion shared by many people throughout the world). We also now see, as was not widely perceived in the 1980s, how decrepit the Soviet economic system was. But the right wing goes much further in its warrant. First, they insist that it was specifically Reagan's military buildup that unhinged Soviet communism, and, second, that the *coup de grâce* of the rearmament was the Strategic Defense Initiative (SDI), Reagan's cherished Star Wars program announced in March 1983.

While Soviet leaders did view the belligerent statements of Reagan, Haig, Jeane Kirkpatrick, and Caspar W. Weinberger with alarm—and were particularly concerned with a possible invasion of Cuba—Soviet military planning did not change appreciably in the early 1980s. In that half-decade, much of the activity in Moscow, which was beset by leadership crises, centered on responding politically to the aggressive stance of the United States. Maneuvers over negotiations and posturing over who was responsible for the deterioration of superpower relations were paramount, but the USSR did not suddenly boost military spending or reshuffle priorities. There was an announced 12 percent increase in spending in 1984, but that appeared to be a response to the public's fears about U.S. intentions and lobbying by the Red Army, and it came after years of flat spending even as the United States was escalating its allocations sharply. Moscow's military production priorities and deployments did not alter, even as Soviet defense intellectuals clearly understood the West's new, high-tech innovations in conventional weaponry. As a number of scholars have concluded after combing the Soviet archives opened in the 1990s, there was no panicky response to the Reagan rearmament that led to Soviet economic or political depletion.[5]

That relatively unruffled response included SDI. Soviet leaders were wary of Reagan's motives for upgrading America's long-standing program to research ballistic missile defense, precisely because it could, if even partially capable, provide the United States with a far more credible first-strike capability. But, again, the Soviets did relatively little (aside from howling about it) in their military preparations. They rightly saw SDI deployment as improbable, and if such a system did come to some sort of fruition, they would respond not by trying to match SDI, but by investing in more ballistic missiles or simple technologies, so-called countermeasures, to defeat it.

As a result, when Gorbachev came to power in March 1985, the Soviets were maintaining the status quo. In fact, it was Reagan who was moving toward a more moderate stance by mid-decade: he fired Haig in 1982, put some far-reaching arms-reduction schemes on the negotiating table in 1983, and made a major, conciliatory speech in January 1984.

The entry of Gorbachev at that moment, then, when there was a slight thaw in relations, argues not for a surrender by the Politburo, but for continuity. In the Soviet records, in fact, there is no indication that Gorbachev appeared to represent anything other than continuity. And that is certainly how he was viewed in the United States.

The reception given to Gorbachev by American opinion elites was uniformly cool and even derisive. While his reformer credentials were already known, he was widely disparaged as another typical Soviet strongman. Within days of Gorbachev's election, Harvard's Marshall Goldman described him as a "a lifelong party member, a product of the system," whose selection "may not be as sharp a departure from past Soviet experience as it first appears." Also in the *New York Times*, Dimitri Simes of the Carnegie Endowment for International Peace warned that "from Nicaragua to Angola, from Syria to Afghanistan, the Kremlin shows no willingness to seek a graceful exit," he wrote just a month after Gorbachev's ascension. "Those who hasten to embrace our Soviet opponents simply because they have a new and more impressive boss live in a world of illusions." Three months later, on the same op-ed page, Simes asserted that "there is nothing in Mikhail Gorbachev's record or his recent statements and actions to suggest that rapprochement with the United States is among his top priorities . . . Already, despite essential continuity, Mr. Gorbachev's foreign policy has been marked by a more assertive, even belligerent, tone." A year after Gorbachev was named general secretary, and following a series of reform and disarmament measures, the *Washington Post* opined that Gorbachev was "something closer to 'Brezhnevism without Brezhnev,' " and that in his devotion to a Soviet system "rigidly centralized under party control . . . [he] remains, in that sense, a Stalinist." The *Times*, at that one-year anniversary, speculated that we "were hearing the same old song from a better singer." And at the end of 1986, after the Reykjavik summit, Robert Kaiser of the *Washington Post* stated that Soviet "leaders remain less interested in international stability than in expanding Soviet influence . . . No foreseeable change in the style or substance of Soviet policies, at home or abroad, will transform our

Soviet problem." This consensus was that of the centrist, even liberal, opinion shapers. The right wing was, of course, even more wary: "The Soviet aim of world domination," wrote an editor of *National Review*, "is not going to vanish. . . . [Gorbachev] may be expected to pursue the standing objective with more energy."[6]

So the political right (and center) of America did not see in Gorbachev's leadership an "act of surrender" or anything like it. Indeed, it was commonly asserted that Gorbachev's apparent interest in restructuring the Soviet economy was to make the Soviet bear more formidable. To the extent he was regarded as a modernizer or reformer—and many saw him as merely media-savvy instead—it was to strengthen the Soviet military to better challenge the West. The Soviets were alleged to possess a formidable strategic defense program of their own, a clear advantage in conventional forces in Europe, equal or possibly even an edge in nuclear weapons, and now a superior propagandist at the helm. So the Soviet Union in the mid to late 1980s was seen by this conventional wisdom as unchanged in essence, still the durable and dangerous superpower.

The claim that the Reagan rearmament and rhetoric made Moscow bow, therefore, is unfounded. Were the Soviets alarmed by loose talk of fighting a nuclear war? Of course. Did they seek to restrain SDI? Naturally. They were interested in the relative stability of nuclear parity that was achieved with the Strategic Arms Limitation Treaty and the Anti-Ballistic Missile (ABM) Treaty. But their actions were quite moderate in response to Reagan's brinksmanship. Until Gorbachev gained full authority in the Kremlin, continuity reigned.

The centrist explanation for the end of the Cold War—that the bipartisan support for containment, both military and diplomatic, finally paid off—is a tautology of sorts, and fails to address the specific causes of the Cold War's demise. In the 1980s, the Democratic House of Representatives approved much of Reagan's policies, even aid to the *contras* in 1986. A number of nuclear arms programs were constrained, notably SDI, but none were terminated. A clever argument could be made that by trimming Reagan's sails, the Democratic leadership brought his policies back to the course of established Cold War policy. When the internal decay in the Soviet Union became unbearable, Gorbachev tried emergency resuscitation but only hastened communism's death. Steadfastness on the part of the United States was a necessary condition for that collapse to occur.

This image of perseverance belies the disarray among many Democrats, and indeed among a large segment of the arms-control community. Centrists took a "we don't and can't know" attitude toward Gorbachev and Soviet intentions, never quite believing that Gorbachev's proposals were anything more than the counterpart of Reagan's own extraordinary public relations. By 1986, many despaired of achieving any arms control, and were deeply suspicious of (and essentially opposed to) the deep cuts proposals coming from the two leaders and the peace movement in Europe and the United States. To the extent that a coherent, moderate position can be recalled, it revolved around nuclear deterrence, which was not only moral, they argued, but virtually sacrosanct. Increasingly, the centrists spoke of modest military procurement reform and investing in avoiding accidental nuclear war as the primary objective, and thereby fashioned themselves "owls" rather than hawks or doves. Many persuaded themselves that Nicaragua and southern Africa really were important venues of superpower competition and that some of the Reagan Doctrine should be supported. And while many in their ranks saw some excesses in U.S. policy, their rhetoric never failed to be cloaked in the terms of U.S. security interests above all else. In other words, smooth the rough edges of Reaganism, but advance the basic tenets of the Cold War. The centrists' claims of playing a leading role in the demise of the superpower competition rest on virtually the same dubious grounds as the right wing's.

THE THIRD WAY: HOW THE PEACENIKS DID IT

Against these sweeping declarations—the intimidating power of Reaganism, or the long, steadfast success of containment—how can the peace movement forward its own claim of success? The case rests on two phenomena. First was the way peace activism created a public demand for an end to the nuclear madness. Second was how a parallel expectation was devised within the new Soviet elite surrounding Gorbachev.

The public demand came in several parts, not so much as a conscious strategy, but as an improvisation that sometimes led and as often responded to events. It began with a calculated effort to stigmatize nuclear weapons, to clarify and amplify the vaguely held notion that these were fundamentally unusable weapons. Between 1980 and 1982, the conventional thinking about nukes went from a shadowy concern about the Russians being "ahead" to abhorrence at the thought of the weapons ever being used. Even Reagan, in this most-hyperbolic phase of his belligerency, was forced to say that the weapons could not be used and that—his administration's doctrine notwithstanding—no winners were possible in a nuclear war. The physicians and scientists did the technical work and raised the alarm, and the growing antinuclear movement (in Europe especially, which saw itself as the helpless victim of both superpowers) provided the mass angst that made the warnings politically potent.

The rise of the nuclear freeze campaign was both an outcome of this growing stigma, and a spur that galvanized further public outrage. Thousands of freeze chapters quickly developed all over the country; its scale was apparent in the June 12, 1982, demonstration in Central Park, the largest ever, when 750,000 people gathered. News media coverage of the movement and its proposals was almost a daily occurrence. It was a citizens movement that in part questioned the very legitimacy of elite decision making, far more than the professionals' groups could (as they were, after all, elites themselves, if no less contentious), and this constituted a threatening political movement. It also stimulated a clamor about the moral validity of deterrence, something the arms-control community was never prepared to do; it drew the voluble support of many clerics, including the Catholic bishops, and innumerable Sunday sermons from Protestant pulpits. This movement was quite a serious challenge, and one that resonated with the American people. Thirty-six nuclear freeze referenda were passed in November 1982. Large demonstrations in Central Park on a sunny summer day, or articles in policy journals were one thing, and possibly negligible; thirty-six victories in thirty-nine referenda—including eight of nine states—was something Washington took to heart.

That this public reproach was transformative can be clearly seen in opinion surveys. In 1981, as Reagan entered office, only about a third of Americans favored the worldwide elimination of nuclear weapons. But by 1983, the number had leaped to four out of every five. Even the deployment of the Euromissiles was viewed suspiciously, with nearly two-thirds favoring a delay to negotiate with the USSR. Support for a nuclear weapons freeze was steady and high, reaching a peak of 86 percent. This sentiment was verified by the obverse: a "get tough" attitude toward Moscow dropped in the public's esteem, from 77 percent in 1980 to just 44 percent in May 1982.

As rapidly expanding distaste for the nuclear rivalry became apparent, the Reagan administration responded. A savvy team headed by a master of persuasion, the White House used every means possible to defeat the freeze referenda, from a public-relations blitz to referring to the antinuclear activists as tools of Moscow. Increasingly, the Reagan administration abandoned its bellicose rhetoric and moved steadily toward serious negotiations with the Soviet Union. "Ronald Reagan came into office on a Republican platform explicitly pledging the new government to achieve 'technological and military superiority' over the Soviet Union," explains David Cortright, a leader of SANE and SANE–Freeze in the 1980s. "Popular culture became increasingly antinuclear as the freeze movement swept the country. Faced with this un-receptive political climate, the Reagan administration largely aban-doned its harsh rhetoric and quietly dropped the concept of superior-ity." Cortright provides one of the few meticulously documented histories of how the Reagan administration responded to the freeze and its allies in his 1993 book, *Peace Works*, and it is apparent from his interviews with top Reagan aides that such bold measures as the strate-gic arms limitation talk (START) proposals and the "zero option" for Euromissiles were stirred significantly by the growing antinuclear ac-tivism in the United States and Europe. Even at the time, it was appar-ent that Reagan's peace offensive was aimed as much at freeze inven-tor Randy Forsberg as Leonid Brezhnev. "Our main concern," a top administration official told the *New York Times* on May 2, 1982, "is to go on the record quickly with a simple and comprehensible plan to show the Reagan team is for peace, thus taking some of the steam out of the nuclear freeze movements in Europe and the United States." Mary Kaldor, a leading historian and activist in England, noted wryly that the zero option idea itself was stolen by Reagan aides from the protes-tors they routinely decried as dupes of Moscow. "I remember having a drink," Kaldor recalled, "with a senior Reagan administration official the night the zero option was announced. 'We got the idea from your banners,' he said, chuckling. 'You know the ones that say 'No Cruise, No Pershing, No SS–20.''' Michael Deaver, Reagan's image maestro, also said the zero option "was our response to the anti-nuke people."[7]

The Reagan White House rarely responded directly to the peace movement; more often, it dealt with a Congress that was increas-ingly aroused by the peace movement. Congress was rather passive on most of Reagan's early initiatives, aside from his provocative pol-icy toward El Salvador and Nicaragua. Then, by the autumn of 1981, the number of initiatives flowing from Congress on nuclear policy mounted quickly to include, over the next few years, unilateral re-straint on antisatellite weapons and SDI testing, curbs on nuclear weapons tests, reductions in Pentagon spending, complex formulas for stabilizing the nuclear deterrent and negotiating cuts with the So-viet Union, and resolutions on the freeze idea itself. It was an aston-ishingly bold assortment of legislation, some of it passing both the Democratic House and a Senate that was Republican until 1987. Con-gress was not only acting to restrain the president, as it did in the 1970s, but actually initiated arms-control policies with far-reaching consequences—as with the space weapons bans.

How did this happen? How could a Congress, wholly pliant on economic policy and cowed by Reagan's anticommunist crusade of 1980–81, suddenly find the gumption to confront an ever-popular president? It is apparent that the outcry represented by the freeze campaign and its public interest allies emboldened Congress to look more skeptically at the "winnable nuclear war" ideas and technologies being promoted by the Reagan administration. As Barry Blechman, then a Brookings scholar, put it, the antinuclear movement "radically altered the political calculus of arms control. Politicians who preferred to forget in 1980 that they ever said a positive word about arms control could not work hard enough two years later to make clear their commitment and support." The Congress "did not originate the freeze movement—far from it . . . It served instead as a conduit, responding to popular concerns about nuclear weapons." The freeze and the professional organizations helped establish a permanent capacity for arms-control initiatives in Congress that lasted well beyond the apogee of activism in the early to mid-1980s.[8]

The House and Senate particularly responded to the technical expertise of scientists on issues of nuclear doctrine, SDI, antisatellite weapons, and related matters, a persuasive power that reshaped political culture far beyond Capitol Hill. It has been suggested that SDI itself was a response to the freeze, a peculiar reflection of Reagan's own doubts about the morality of mutually assured destruction. Whatever SDI's origin, the scientists' disapproval—especially the technical critiques that revealed it to be an extremely improbable prospect—was one of the decade's most decisive episodes. First came the broad critique by the Union of Concerned Scientists (UCS), whose team included Nobel laureates and weapons scientists like Hans Bethe, Richard Garwin, and Henry Kendall, then similar appraisals from several other institutes. The news media were receptive to the scientists' broadsides, and, as a result, the public never wholly bought in to Reagan's dream. Large numbers (*e.g.*, 48 percent in October 1984) believed it would escalate the arms race, and occasionally even large majorities deemed it too expensive to deploy—ideas that came directly from the professional opposition. But the sheer complexity of SDI made public opinion a difficult read. What was more solidly anti–SDI was elite appraisals: Very few independent scientists favored the program, and hundreds spoke out against it, which was reflected among opinion leaders (the *New York Times* in particular) and in Congress, which routinely limited the administration's grandiose plans despite the obvious pork barrel possibilities of the program. By early 1985, when Gorbachev rose in the Kremlin, several panels of leading American scientists had stoutly declaimed Star Wars as an unworkable—yet dangerous—addition to the nuclear rivalry, one that the Soviets could easily counter but would nonetheless view (rightly) as mounting a potential first-strike threat against them.

By that pivotal moment, virtually no one in policy-responsible circles believed that SDI as articulated by Reagan was a plausible concept.

When Gorbachev and Reagan started their slow dance in the summit meetings, the contours of American attitudes were already rather firmly set. The public, at first alarmed by the possibility of nuclear war, then upset by the "externalities" of the Cold War—the costs, the hazards of the weapons complex, the moral corruption of the Central American imbroglio—sustained their distaste well beyond the salad days of the freeze campaign. The public and elites of all kinds wanted better relations with the Soviets and were pressing to cut nuclear weapons, SDI, and conventional forces in Europe. This agenda was manifestly different from what Reagan set out achieve. It was vastly more far-reaching than what the Democratic leadership articulated in 1980–81. It was, indeed, more assertive and visionary than the old arms-control cliques proposed through most of the 1980s. As my colleague Matt Fellowes notes in a study of public opinion: "in 1986, 80 percent were in favor of a nuclear test ban, 82 percent were against weapons in space, and 84 percent were in favor of reducing Soviet and U.S. warheads by 50 percent." Despite Reagan's popularity, "the public remained highly supportive of arm-control negotiations, and increasingly opposed to further defense spending. This point became clearer by the mid-1980s, when the public clearly had begun to withdraw support for further nuclear development and militarization, while maintaining high levels of support for continued arms-control negotiations. This trend developed despite increasingly confrontational rhetoric from the White House and near-record lows in American feelings about the Soviets."[9]

A highly symbolic reckoning in the decade came at the Reykjavik summit in late 1986. This summit is where Reagan and Gorbachev nearly agreed to total nuclear disarmament, but for Reagan's emotional attachment to the Star Wars fantasy. Many among the foreign policy elite were aghast at Reagan's "near miss" in Iceland, convinced (erroneously) as they were of Soviet conventional superiority in Europe. The conservative parties running much of Western Europe were shaken, having spent so much political capital (and actual pounds, marks, and francs) on the absolute need for nuclear deterrence; and Reagan's own chief adviser would call his nuclear abolitionism "dangerous rubbish."[10] But the American president and the Soviet Communist boss nearly did what only the most brazen peaceniks had been proposing—get rid of the nukes. The fact that these two implacable foes could come within a hair's breadth of eliminating their colossal nuclear arsenals was a testament to their own sense of responsibility for the survival of civilization, forged in the specter of nuclear winter, the horrifying consequences of the Chernobyl accident, and the escalating, worldwide demand for action to reduce the nuclear danger.

Reykjavik also led to the next moment emblematic of the demise of the Cold War—the signing of the Intermediate Nuclear Forces (INF) Treaty in 1987. Reagan had been crippled by the Iran-*contra* scandal, which threatened for a time to bring down his presidency. He responded by moving closer toward Gorbachev. (That Reagan was winging it on his own, for political reasons, is apparent from an examination of administration documents from the period, which were as belligerently Cold War as ever.[11]) The INF agreement was the first major consequence of Reagan's transformation, signed just a year after the Iran-*contra* scandal became public. The zero option, accursed by conservatives and many arms controllers alike because it supposedly "decoupled" U.S. and European nuclear security, became the first major arms-reduction treaty of the 1980s. It was opposed by Senate majority leader Robert Byrd and Representative Les Aspin, both key Democrats, and numerous others in Washington's higher circles, including Kissinger, Richard Nixon, and Brent Scowcroft. But the overwhelming public approval for the treaty—more than 80 percent—collapsed the opposition within weeks. And this public approval was clearly a triumph of peace activism. The European movement in particular had also called for a zero option; the Democratic Party was ambivalent, at best, about it; and conservatives opposed it. The INF agreement, ratified by the Senate in 1988, was the first payoff for the sustained and clamorous public demand for an end to nuclear madness. Later that year, the odd couple of Gorbachev and Reagan sketched what would eventually become the two Strategic Arms Reduction Treaties, which dramatically cut into strategic nuclear arsenals, another move that earned enthusiastic approval from the American public.

How the "cousin" movement to prevent intervention in Central America affected the end of the Cold War is harder to gauge. Despite the importance attached to Nicaragua and El Salvador by Reagan, Haig, and Kirkpatrick, Gorbachev readily discarded it as a point of contention. What the long struggle over U.S. policy did do was to depreciate the hyperbolic claims of the Reaganites about communism. Most Americans never believed the notion that Sandinistas represented a national security threat to the United States. Coupled with obvious, false piety toward the *contras* and the junta in El Salvador, including tolerance of their outrageous human rights conduct, this rhetoric significantly devalued the moral sanctity of anticommunism. The Reagan assault in Central America, often illegal and almost always immoral, hollowed out the residual American distrust of all things communist and made it easier for peace activists to successfully argue for a deep and abiding detente.

That the detente came at all, of course, was due in no small measure to the ascent of Gorbachev. But long before March 1985, the peace movement in the West had succeeded brilliantly at "changing the conversation" about the morality of nuclear weapons, the nature of East-West relations, and the ill effects of the Cold War. Thomas Rochon notes with respect to Europe that "the peace movement was the agent behind the transformation of the INF issue from being a policy decided primarily on military grounds by a few political leaders and technical experts to being a massively debated issue invested with political meaning."[12] And that transformation describes the American disarmament crusade as well, one that captured, and held hostage, the discourse on nuclear weapons for nearly a decade.

THE ECHO EFFECT

Perhaps the more remarkable part of the story, however, is how the public demand for change in the West was echoed in Moscow, with tangible results then replayed on the world stage. The steady parade to the Soviet Union and Eastern European satillites by ordinary citizen diplomats, lawyers, doctors, scientists, and a variety of dissident politicians created an entirely different—and largely unanticipated—dynamic for detente. At one level, all this contact merely turned up the volume of popular clamor in Western capitals by broadcasting the peace agenda from different venues. Someone like Dr. Bernard Lown could say precisely the same thing in Moscow as he said in Boston, but with a Russian physician at his side, after a meeting with a Soviet leader, his message carried more weight. This simple, self-induced echoing was the most plentiful East-West activity among nonprofit groups, practiced by a veritable deluge of sister city envoys, caravans of students, delegations of this union or that recreation club, ad infinitum. These forays had one salient virtue: They raised the temperature on politicians in Europe and in the United States, a constant reminder that a popular will was escalating. When the local Rotary Club president visits Moscow, sees an apparent desire for better relations, and returns to telephone the local newspaper editor and member of Congress, that is retail democracy at its most vigorous; repeated thousands of times—as it was—it sends an unmistakable message.

This seemingly spontaneous outbreak of citizen diplomacy also touched Eastern Europe, particularly Poland, Czechoslovakia, Hungary, and East Germany. The political dynamics were different, of course. Even before Reagan was elected, the labor union Solidarity had already made its astonishing and formidable challenge in Poland in 1980, a revolt not just of the unions but of civil society and clerics, which served as a touchstone for the remainder of the decade. Political dissent was rife in the other "captive" nations, and was championed more and more by dissidents in the West; the specter of Soviet repression in Hungary in 1956 and Czechoslovakia in 1968 haunted social democrats. From an early stage of the antinuclear protests, efforts were mounted to connect to the human rights activists in the Warsaw Pact countries, and another unlikely alliance was forged, one that saw the nuclear madness and repression as part of the same loathsome superpower manipulation. This bridge building was much more an undertaking of Europeans than Americans, and was certainly not confined to the political left (the Catholic Church played an enormous role). But it served to starkly expose a dimension of the Cold War that had only sporadically earned attention over the previous four decades—the tenuous and clumsy, if no less contemptible grip of Soviet communism on these Eastern Europeans.

Possibly the most consistently influential echo effect was that created by "policy entrepreneurs" that engaged the Kremlin over a number of years. Chief among these were scientists who began to engage their Soviet counterparts very early in the Cold War, and whose access and persuasive powers grew steadily. The most notable of these was Pugwash, an organization of scientists from around the world that met regularly, formed working groups, issued papers, and the like from the 1950s on. By the 1980s, Pugwash-convened task forces had addressed the whole range of arms issues besetting the superpower rivalry—nuclear testing, ballistic missile defense, conventional forces, and nuclear doctrine—and provided Soviet scientists with insights on arms control that they may not have found elsewhere. By the early 1980s, the Pugwash group was supplemented by several others: Frank von Hippel and Jeremy Stone of the Federation of American Scientists, Manhattan Project physicist Victor Weiskopf, Tom Cochran of the Natural Resources Defense Council (NRDC), Bernard Lown of the International Physicians for the Prevention of Nuclear War, Randy Forsberg of the Institute for Defense and Disarmament Studies, and many more.

The policy entrepreneurs went to Moscow for any number of reasons, typically to create some sense of momentum towards arms control that would resonate back in the United States. What was less expected was how hungrily the Soviets would take up their suggestions for arms restraint and the "new thinking" inherent in the American and European peace community. The Soviet policy elite, beginning in the Brezhnev era but flowering, of course, under Gorbachev, adopted several of the most important initiatives of the Western activists. Among the more penetrating influences was the Palme Commission, which argued at length in 1982 for a "common security" framework in which the security of one's adversary becomes a key consideration in one's own defense thinking. "The work in the Palme Commission began a very important stage in my life," a top Kremlin adviser, Georgi Arbatov, wrote years later, "and exerted a major influence on my understanding of politics and international relations." It is worth noting that a number of Soviet "influentials," including Arbatov, Georgi Shaknazarov, Fyodor Burlatsky, and Evgeni Velikov, among others, were closet reformers from an early stage, and helped pave the way for "Western" ideas. (There was also a social movement in the USSR, not state-controlled, which exerted some useful pressure on the Communist Party.) Nonetheless, the entire complex of peace researchers working on new, nonoffensive concepts of security—led by Anders Boserup in Denmark, Egon Bahr and Lutz Unterseher in West Germany, and Randy Forsberg in the United States—apparently had a profound influence on the Russians that extended beyond conventional forces to nuclear doctrine.[13] The thinking seeped in through many pores in the membrane of Soviet communism, notably through the scientists' exchanges (Pugwash, for example, had a working group on conventional forces), the many intellectual forums sponsored by peace groups, and through the influence exerted by particular Soviet officials who later became prominent in Gorbachev's inner circle. The interest shown and the changes made as a result of these rich, sustained contacts belies the right-wing view of the Soviet Union at that time as rigidly monolithic and unchangeable. The more realistic assessment, ironically, came from the more utopian thinkers of the peace community—they saw the possibility of change, and their collective hunch was correct. The fundamental idea put forward, moreover, that one could enhance one's own security not by threatening one's adversaries but by reassuring them, was simple but sophisticated. Unlike many philosophical platitudes of left or right, it was one that could be manifested in military procurement, deployments, and strategy.

The Soviets applied this idea, gradually but steadily, throughout the 1980s. Moscow's embrace of common security concepts accounts for the firm attitude that nuclear arsenals should be eliminated or drastically cut. The nuclear testing moratorium, unilaterally pursued by Moscow in 1986–87, was an early, concrete expression of this view; it was aided magnificently by the NRDC seismic monitoring project, which not only bolstered the public relations value of the test ban but actually influenced Gorbachev's thinking about issues of nuclear stockpile maintenance, verification, and the like. In the crucial realm of conventional forces, Boserup, his British associate Robert Nield, and others (including Americans Forsberg and von Hippel) directly lobbied Gorbachev to explore the new concepts of nonoffensive defense. The result of this lobbying and many other such intellectual inroads was the 1988 draft treaty to reduce and reconfigure conventional forces in Europe, tabled by the Soviets in the Vienna talks with the United States. It was, in all important respects, a nonoffensive defense design, a radical departure from previous Soviet positions. So, too, were the unilateral reductions in conventional forces in Eastern Europe in late 1988, especially significant since Gorbachev pledged before the United Nations that December not to intervene in the affairs of other Warsaw Pact countries—fateful declarations, given the events of late 1989. Soviet officials also credited Boserup and others with a central role in the U.S.–USSR talks leading to the Conventional Forces in Europe Treaty in 1990.

Similarly, the scientist-diplomats convinced Gorbachev to abandon the Soviet position of demanding that the United States halt Star Wars before reductions in nuclear-tipped missiles could be bargained for. Von Hippel and Stone, given their access to Gorbachev, were essential agents of this message, but it was also a view widely held among the most prestigious scientists in the West and readily conveyed to their Soviet counterparts through innumerable visits, forums, books, articles, and so forth. By the time the issue was decided, the thundering critique of SDI in America had resonated throughout Moscow. Notably, it was an opinion strongly held by Andrei Sakharov, the legendary Soviet physicist who was a stalwart critic of SDI and who had played an important role in moving Moscow to embrace the ABM Treaty in 1972. SDI was viewed warily, of course, but it was neither an official obsession nor a spur to reform. It was a nettlesome alteration of the deterrence and arms-control formulae, but one that could be handled "asymmetrically" (*i.e.*, that SDI could be defeated by simple countermeasures, as UCS had first stated in 1984). Ironically, it may have been the dissident Sakharov's judgment that there was no near-term danger to the Soviet deterrent that proved decisive. He had informed Soviet officials of the need to separate SDI from arms-reduction talks as early as 1986, and gave a speech asserting that position to a huge, East-West peace forum in Moscow in February 1987, at which Gorbachev was present. Gorbachev soon after announced the de-linking of SDI to arms reductions, and the INF Treaty and the START draft soon followed.[14] Gorbachev's public position on Star Wars reflected the view of many of the American scientists who opposed the program: If you want to eliminate the threat of nuclear weapons, then eliminate nuclear weapons.

Throughout this process, the many peace researchers and activists involved in this astonishing scheme made concerted efforts to relay the good news of Moscow's depth of change to Western capitals. Both Russians and those from the West were involved in this process, briefing policy and opinion leaders and introducing new twists to each extraordinary Gorbachev gambit. By 1989, even before the Berlin Wall was a target of German chisels, the West had essentially surrendered to Gorbachev's entreaties.

For all explanations of the end of the Cold War, Gorbachev is pivotal. What actually motivated him, then, and how his actions were formulated is crucial. Clearly, the proposals and arguments of the "policy entrepreneurs" were exceptionally influential. This phenomenon is illuminated by Cornell professor Matthew Evangelista's 1999 book, *Unarmed Forces: The Transnational Movement to End the Cold War*, a thorough and scholarly exploration that delved into the Soviet archives for answers. He concludes that Gorbachev "seemed to welcome transnational contacts—and not only on technical issues of nuclear arms control. He paved the way for transnational activists to challenge the Soviet military's competence within their core domain of planning for conventional warfare in Europe. The influences of foreign scientists and peace activists in preparing the intellectual ground for ending the East-West military standoff in central Europe contributed much to the peaceful demise of the Cold War."[15]

The ingredients contributing to the demise of the U.S.–Soviet rivalry are too numerous, too intertwined, and too enigmatic to gauge with absolute confidence. The proponents of Reagan's "victory" have some valid points, as does the centrists' emphasis on containment. A full rendering of the topic would have to account for a large number of disconnected factors as well: the Polish pontiff, the accident at Chernobyl, oil prices, the growing prosperity of Western Europe, the penetration of new consumer technologies, and even influences like rock 'n' roll.

The rivalry was also a multifaceted affair, one of ideology and culture and political styles. First and foremost, however, it was one of armaments. The U.S.–Soviet confrontation was, by the mid-1960s, a highly formalized conflict, attended by vast bureaucracies of arms making and arms control, strategists for war-making and strategists for coexistence, with universities, laboratories, institutes, and manufacturers all in place to sustain it. Only something extraordinary could break up this powerful, self-perpetuating colossus. Reagan, with his eccentric blend of utter stupidity and deft political acuity, was very much in the tradition of the American Cold Warrior—the bad cop, the anticommunist crusader, the pro-military commander in chief. Even SDI was just a twist on a very old theme. It took something more radical, more disruptive and normative, to crack the ice of the Cold War.

That disruption was brandished in the cacophonous demand for an end to the nuclear madness that resonated first throughout Europe and then quickly in the United States. It found a soul mate of sorts in the new Soviet leader who somehow opened his mind to new ideas for disarmament and cooperation. That the peace movement stood at both ends of this triumph, creating a loud and persistent echo from West to East and back again, is one of the great achievements of the twentieth century.

5

DID PHILANTHROPY
MAKE A DIFFERENCE?

Two days before Thanksgiving 1991, just five weeks before the Cold War "officially" ended with the final demise of the Soviet Union, a large group of foundation executives met in the splendid conference room of the Rockefeller Foundation in New York. The meeting was typical of those I had attended—mainly useful as information exchange, since nothing like a common strategy was seriously discussed. In the midst of a go-around in which each donor at the long table spoke to current concerns, I mentioned that our community of activists and researchers had profoundly influenced the end of the Cold War. This statement elicited a quizzical look from one of the group's major donors, who then asked what I meant. I replied briefly that the peace movement had spoken up for disarmament and detente at a time when no prominent politicians dared to, and had made the goal of nuclear arms reductions a standard of political debate throughout the 1980s. The room was quiet as I spoke, and I could see in the faces of my colleagues that few either understood what I was saying or could locate the same sense of achievement.

On the train ride back to Boston, I puzzled over the peculiar reaction to my mild assertion. True, the people present that day had not been, for the most part, the activist-oriented funders of the early 1980s. But the blank response, I thought, reflected a disappointment as well, an absence of conviction in what I believed had been gained. I recalled another moment, in 1988, speaking to my friend Richard Healey, then the publisher of the movement magazine, *Nuclear Times*. It was a few days before Gorbachev was to visit Washington to sign the first nuclear arms-reduction agreement, the Intermediate Nuclear Forces (INF) Treaty. I said to Richard, why not throw a party to celebrate our victory? Invite Gorbachev and Reagan. His ironic reply was that no one in our peace community felt much like celebrating.

The movement was in the doldrums even as its first, brilliant accomplishment was about to be codified at a White House ceremony.

While these two anecdotes scarcely represent a fair survey of attitudes, they do reflect the dashed hopes of many in the peace movement. The expectations of the activists, intellectuals, and donors after their vast antinuclear movement burst onto the world stage were high, and even the nuclear reductions under way by 1991 did not seem to satisfy them. Still, with the value of temporal distance, it seems apparent—as argued in the last chapter—that the achievements of peace research and activism in the 1980s were prodigious.

If the peace movement was a decisive factor in ending the Cold War, then it's reasonable to conclude that American philanthropy, as the movement's sugar daddy, can take some credit for the great transformation of 1980–91. The funders directly backed the specific causes of change: the alarms about the effects of nuclear war; the broad, public clamor for an end to the arms race; the steady drumbeat about the excessive costs of the Cold War; the policy entrepreneurs dealing with Soviet elites; and the media attention given to those issues. In each of these efforts, funders were present, often as prominent instigators. But the record is murky, clouded not only by the perception of failure, but by the absence of a sense of strategy. The lesson one draws should pivot less on expectations, perhaps, than what was achieved and how.

THE WINNING TEAM

Weighing donor influence is always complex, and very little about matters of war and peace in the 1980s conformed to straightforward causality. The success was so extraordinary, and the extent of change so unexpected, that one searches for intentionality where, perhaps, none existed. The cause-and-effect of this historic change—the ways and means of donor influence in the ending of the Cold War—are nonetheless suggestible. Equally significant, of course, is the precise nature of causation, the way it was created and sustained, its limitations and mistakes.

The simple case is made by matching the causes of change to the presence of early and indispensable investment by donors. This process is a fairly easy thing to do. Probably the most obvious case is the earliest period—especially the funding of the Physicians for Social Responsibility (PSR) in 1979–81. Helen Caldicott's take-no-prisoners road show was a catalytic phenomenon like few others in the history of social movements, and the donors who backed her early on often made an enormous difference in PSR's ability to alert and mobilize vast numbers so quickly.

The second example is the Nuclear Weapons Freeze Campaign. Randy Kehler, the national coordinator of the freeze, credits donors like Wade Greene, Jay Harris, Ed Lawrence, and Bob Allen with timely, leveraging grants that greatly and quickly expanded the capacity of the national office. One senses that the freeze movement would have occurred regardless of the actions of the donor community—in part because so much of the freeze phenomenon was voluntary and local—but its rapid expansion and its preeminence as the pivot point of peace activism was enabled by large sums of donor money. Likewise, the withholding of grants after 1984 accelerated its decline. "After three years, the funding began to fall off," recalls Kehler. "It coincided with the loss of political momentum. SDI, the attacks on us as having been influenced by the KGB, those hurt us. When we needed the money most, it wasn't there. That's not to say that had the money been there, things would have been different." But the upside is the earlier period of the freeze's immense impact on American political culture; says Meg Gage, who was close to the freeze as a donor and participant: "The freeze would not have been as powerful without foundation money. Funders were huge in the success of the freeze; you can't even calculate it."

The third case is that of professionalization. The donors invested substantially in the assemblies of physicians, educators, scientists, psychologists, economists, lawyers, *et alia,* and by the time the freeze was sliding away, these groups were poised for a leading role. Likewise, the college peace-studies programs, led by Michael Klare's Five College consortium in Amherst, Massachusetts, had grown rapidly, providing action and expertise throughout the United States. This rich, dense mixture of local and national elites, interdisciplinary approaches, and the politically potent norm of "social responsibility" was very much an intentional strategy of foundations and private donors. It was attractive not only on its merits, but because it permitted many foundations not accustomed to activist funding to participate. "We funded PSR, the international physicians group, the Federation of American Scientists (Jeremy Stone played the board like an accordion), and other professional groups," says John Redick, who headed the W. Alton Jones Foundation in the early 1980s. "They were blossoming like roses in the spring. We found that easy going with our board." As one observer puts it, the grants for professional groups provided a "cover" for the cautious, tradition-bound philanthropies to get involved. "The professionals were a way of broadening elite involvement, and that was brilliant," says Rob Stein, the Forum Institute's director in the early 1980s. "That came from Bob Scrivner."

Finally, the policy entrepreneurs who went to Moscow to inform and embolden the Soviet advisers to Gorbachev were very much the

beneficiaries of philanthropy. Travel costs alone made such sizable donations a necessity. Frank von Hippel was a favorite, given his visionary reach, scientific skill, and easygoing personality, a rare combination
in the prickly world of physicists. NRDC was another. Both could
demonstrate close and productive ties to Soviet policy makers. Here,
too, the large foundations with their technical orientation could and
did play a big role. "I was always trying to support Pugwash," says
Ruth Adams, who had been a member for years before heading
MacArthur's program. "Pugwash was really the educators of the Soviet scientists on arms control, and they learned how to negotiate from
Pugwash." The Nobel laureate for peace, Joseph Rotblat, who co-
founded Pugwash with Bertrand Russell, remembers that for many
years they ran it "on a shoestring, sometimes operating from my
home," but how it became easier over time to raise money from foundations like MacArthur, Ford, W. Alton Jones, and the Joseph Rowntree
Trust, a British donor.

In all these phases and tactics—alarm, mobilization, information, and exchanges—the donor community was frequently in a crucial place to make things happen. They were not always the same
donors, and not always giving for similar reasons. But their presence
at each stage and each decisive venue is indisputable. "To inform
and excite is philanthropy's role," explains Rob Stein. "To make social change, it takes ten years to incubate, excite, and get adopted.
The peace movement was ten years in the making, then 1989 came.
The investments of a few financiers made possible these changes, altering the context for the end of the Cold War."

THE PERCEPTION OF FAILURE

Among the more fascinating aspects of the performance of peace
philanthropy was a widespread sense of failure among donors and a
handful of other observers. This feeling was evident to me a number
of times over late 1980s, but the gloom was particularly thick during
that dispiriting donors meeting at the Rockefeller Foundation in late
1991. Now, more than a decade since the Berlin Wall was toppled,
that attitude is just as apparent.

"Well, we survived," was Cora Weiss's pithy response to my
question. And to some degree, this response encapsulates that view,
held by perhaps half the relevant donors, that an untarnished
achievement could not be seen. Two kinds of self-criticism generally
are voiced: first, that the impact of the peace donors was minimal;
and second, that the strategy was misguided.

"Did we have an impact? I guess not," says David Hunter. "That's a terrible thing to say. It seems to me that nuclear weaponry is still a viable policy"—which is another theme, that at century's end, the trajectory of nuclear disarmament apparent in 1989 was not sustained. In that sense then, one's answer depends on what moment in history one regards as the most relevant to judge effectiveness. Similarly, Leslie Dunbar, who not only headed the Field Foundation in the 1970s but was a trustee of the Winston Foundation and the Ruth Mott Fund, brought to my attention at the last Winston board meeting in June 1999 a trenchant criticism of peace activism: that it had failed to change the way policy is made. Such reform was an explicit goal of the activist movement, less so of the experts, of course, and while some new openness and democratic oversight (via Congress) was gained, the sum of this reform is paltry. "Except for the Freedom of Information Act, there's been little progress on this," says Dick Boone, Dunbar's successor at Field. "Congressional oversight is fraudulent."

But even the more basic question—did donors and the groups they supported help end the Cold War?—earns very mixed responses. "I think Reagan beggared the 'evil empire,' " says Ed Lawrence of the Veatch Program. "The publicity about nuclear weapons was effective in making them an unacceptable nuclear option. No question the public attitude was against nuclear confrontation. That was effective work. But did this have an effect on the end of the Cold War? No." Ping Ferry, well before the end of the Cold War was in sight, lamented that "the main difficulty of the movement itself [is] that it is an effective if congenitally disorganized anti-militarism movement," not interested in complete nuclear disarmament *per se*, and in this lack of vision—which afflicted funders as well—an obvious failure.[1]

A more churlish view is offered by Colin Greer, who succeeded Dave Ramage at the New World Foundation in 1984, a post he still holds. "The donors didn't accomplish much," he says now. "There was a movement out there and the donors responded to that, trying to influence the life and direction of the organizations, and pushing other groups, like the Children's Defense Fund, to be attentive to the nuclear issue with additional grants. The Reagan election in 1980 produced a sense of marginality that professional donors had not experienced in twenty years. They wanted to connect to something powerful, and the freeze and meetings with celebrities like Cyrus Vance or Jonathan Schell gave that to them. When the first range of organizations didn't meet their expectations, they drifted away. It was such a passing moment, the public demand for disarmament, and the national security state learned that it could withstand this enormous outpouring."

Much of the despair about influence stems, I believe, from two factors: the disastrous decision of the freeze to work closely with the Walter Mondale campaign in 1984, after which the freeze itself quickly declined; and the fact that the Cold War ended on Reagan's watch (actually George Bush's, but in the role of caretaker), in ways quite unexpected, seeming to be as much an outburst of human rights activism in Eastern Europe as anything else. Both of these phenomena stripped the donor community of its thin veneer of consensus: It is relatively easy to maintain a sense of unity and success when a movement is expanding quickly, especially one that saw itself as a "big tent." Only when things start to go wrong, when hopes are dashed or events take weird turns, do the differences surface. Because so many donors came to fund disarmament work for different reasons, very often without a strong idea of how change was actually going to occur, those unfulfilled expectations began to feel like disappointments. And this problem again goes to the heart of strategies for social change.

THE ACCIDENTAL PURPOSE

Most striking about the self-analysis of the donors from that period is not the occasional note of negativity, but the casualness of their thinking about social change. This pattern emerges not only from the reminiscences of how they viewed strategy at the time, but the disagreements about what should have been done instead.

Nearly all spoke of their grant decisions as being responses to opportunities, for the most part, rather than the implementation of a specific strategy. "We could support popular opposition, the freeze and its theme," says Wade Greene, "and also all the elite arms-control groups. There was not a hell of a lot more thought than that going into it." Another representative statement was Hilary Palmer's: "there wasn't a whole lot of philosophy behind this." To some extent, a donor must choose a very broad category of interest, such as Central America or nuclear nonproliferation, and then choose again among the players already in the field. The "strategy" then depends on the grantee's sense of what will work. Funder-initiated projects, of which there are many examples, are frequently criticized as having no "market test," and many of them are failures. (News media projects seemed to be favorites in this respect.) The most obvious alternative is to cobble together a strategy with what is already available.

While I did believe in articulating a strategy of social change with my trustees—prompted, in fact, by Meg Gage at the Peace Development Fund—I also believed in what I call the "best athlete" option. Borrowing a metaphor from the professional football draft, in which coaches often say they're not filling a specific need but simply drafting the best athlete, I would look for the most capable people within a range of categories—grassroots activists, media specialists, inventive thinkers, et cetera—and fund them under the assumption that something useful would result. In the fog of war, to borrow another image, it's difficult to devise and implement a strategy in which one can have high confidence, particularly when the amounts being spent are modest. Several other donors expressed a similar tendency. "The Hunter group was looking for leadership and trusted it," Harriet Barlow explains. "Give money to people who sense political opportunity, and give them $25,000, a lot of money in 1980. Or give institutional funding to start a campaign." Colin Greer agrees: "The biggest gain from the anti-nuclear funding was that a generation gained experience in political activism, which in turn helped make the environmental movement happen a decade later."

In a similar vein, Ed Lawrence was mindful of fostering durability. "Some donors like David Hunter gave early to projects, he could identify the good ones early, but he didn't stay in. We did stay in. It takes three to five years before you could tell if you were accomplishing anything. There was a much greater possibility of making a mistake by underfunding than by overfunding something." The disagreements over such matters as the wisdom of multiyear funding, or the endless debate about "core" funding (for rent, accounting, administrators, and so on) versus program funding (for the research, advocacy, or public education activities), seem relatively minor compared with larger matters of strategy, but they are the bread-and-butter of movements, and they ultimately affect how easily bold thinking can be carried out. "Most donors wanted to build a movement," Meg Gage argues, "but looked for outcomes that were programmatic rather than organizational." Not willing often enough to provide core support, donors unwittingly created quicksilver organizations that could not easily adapt to a rapidly changing circumstances.

This controversy over how or whether to construct a sturdy infrastructure for peace advocacy erupted in numerous ways. "The funders made a big mistake in 'letting a thousand flowers bloom,'" says Wayne Jaquith. "They spread the money very widely. There were 8,000 grassroots groups and 1,000 national groups, many of them one personality deep. That was disastrous. It meant neutering each group with administrative tasks. The 'teeth to tail' ratio was very low. At a similar moment in the civil rights movement, the funders demanded consolidation and cooperation." But others disagree on that score. "I think that criticism is a cop-out," Harriet Barlow answers. "People weren't willing to see a fresh face or a new idea. That is a very ahistorical way of approaching the work. What we needed was more rigorous analysis of how to accomplish what we wanted."

To some degree this argument is a glass half-full or half-empty. Robert Karl Manoff, who founded and headed the Center for War, Peace, and the News Media, points out that "one real achievement of the funders was the creation of a segment of civil society dedicated to a watchdog role on national security. Compare the coverage of nuclear issues in the '80s with the coverage of the bombing of Hiroshima, which was almost totally statist. Now there is an institutional basis for countervailing voices, something Ford started to do globally in the 1960s. This capacity depends on foundations, and it really took off in the 1980s."

Another contentious element of strategy was how deeply to go into electoral politics and congressional lobbying. A dominant criticism of the freeze was its decision to challenge Reagan in the 1984 presidential election. A number of prominent peaceniks staked the credibility of the disarmament program on popular acceptance first through the attempt to legislate a freeze in Congress, and then through the election of Mondale. The Capitol Hill gambit yielded disappointing results in 1983. "We got stars in our eyes," says Randy Kehler, "when [Senators] Kennedy and Hatfield came to us in our infancy." The election experience—in which $6 million was raised and thousands of activists mobilized through Freeze Voter, a political action committee—was pursued because so many urged the movement to "do politics," to strive for actual political power after the symbolic victories of the 1982 referenda and high poll ratings for the freeze. "Some saw the freeze as a mass movement that could be mobilized against Ronald Reagan in 1984," Colin Greer argues. "But just joining a political campaign is to give away your power. Other electoral strategies could have been pursued."

But many saw the freeze as a wasting asset, gripped by political entropy after its 1980–82 "moment"—however important—had passed. "The freeze was amazing, a huge movement," Rob Stein says. "It had a lot of feet, with no body, and it never wanted a head." Dick Boone, one of the advocates of doing politics, explains that "I became somewhat disenchanted with the freeze; it was not using the power it had to influence the political process. The question was, how do you affect presidential and congressional power? That led me to the political process. There is reticence in the nonprofit world to do any politics out of misplaced fear that it is somehow illegal." He supported in the final years of the Field Foundation such allowable activities as voter education, voter registration, and get-out-the-vote, possibly more than any other foundation, and this momentum continues to this day, a function taken up by the Forum Institute.

The judgment on the freeze's involvement in the 1984 campaign is largely a negative one, but not because social movements should *never* engage in politics. "Freeze Voter and the Mondale campaign destroyed the movement," says Richard Healey, who now heads the Preamble Collaborative in Washington. "Social movements tend to be self-marginalizing and fail to realize that elections and legislation are the payoff. But without organizational power, it can't be done."

The donors had not banked the electoral strategy as wholeheartedly as it did congressional lobbying; in part due to tax-law restrictions, the electoral work is more the province of individual donors than foundations. But the lobbying efforts on behalf of the freeze were, in effect, a popular item for the donor community. As noted in the last chapter, the peace movement's decision to swarm over Capitol Hill had a transformative effect on Congress, an effect sustained by the professionals' coalitions later in the decade and to some degree in the 1990s. The weakness of the freeze resolution itself has masked the profound impact of a new lobbying power, some of it largely permanent, which was created in that period to forward the freeze proposals and other legislation. Not only were key organizations with lobbying dexterity supported, but the funders insisted on cooperation among them, leading to the Monday Lobbying Group meetings at which legislative priorities would be hammered out—much like what was occurring with the groups focused on Central America. There was also a Directors' Forum to enhance communication, although this was a narrowly constructed group. This legislative impulse was built by donors, large and small. It was an intentional piece of strategy (although some were squeamish about violating IRS rules), perhaps the most clear-minded tactic adopted broadly by the donors in the 1980s.

What made lobbying effective, of course, was the public outcry against the nuclear danger, and helping to stir this outcry was also intentional, if far less precise. The outcry itself, and the apparent conformity among donors that such an outcry was appropriate, was at least partially a function of self-interest. "What occasioned the unity," observes Barbara Dudley, the director of the Veatch Program from 1987–91, "was that the Establishment was horrified by what they allowed to happen—that is, the threat of total destruction." And the more traditional foundations could play ball because, in Richard Healey's words, "civic participation is okay as long as the status quo is not challenged, and the nuclear movement did not challenge the class issue, the basic economic structure of the United States."

Still, the movement went a long way toward confronting the militarization that seemed out of control. The economic rationales for arms production, jobs, and exports; the veil of secrecy in foreign and military policy making; the political uses—often illegal—of anticommunism; the morality of U.S. military intervention in the Third World; the neurotic dependency on the nuclear complex, both civil and military; and the fundamental insanity of the nuclear arms race were topics widely and persistently debated in American political culture, all due to the efforts of the peace movement. And, for the most part, this discourse was consciously backed by the peace donors.

The judgment about effectiveness often misreads what social movements can achieve. "By changing social values, movements expand the range of ideas about what is possible," writes Thomas Rochon. "This ultimately has an effect on politics because it changes perceptions of what the most important political problems are. Movements find new solutions to old problems, find new problems, or bring problems from the private realm into the public realm. Movements redefine the political and social environment."[2] Had the freeze and like-minded organizations (*e.g.*, the church-based groups) sustained their function as a *movement*, in contrast to a lobbying group, their impact may have reached much further, to such things as how policy was made. But here the question, probably unanswerable, is whether peace activism, circa 1984, could sustain both its forward thrust as a social movement and convert some of its energy into a savvy, Washington player.

To a significant degree, the dynamics of disarmament activism as a movement—its strengths, potential, need for coalition, et cetera—were not well understood by donors. Here the structure of philanthropy is particularly limiting. Staffs tend to be isolated from others, and even when they are brought together, they rarely feel empowered to act because they must sell program ideas to their boards. The riskier the program, the more barriers they see. Boards themselves, drawn largely from the benefactors' families or from elite circles, typically have even less contact with other donors, are ignorant of any notion of how change happens, or tend to regard program decisions in proprietary ways. The levels of cooperation, then, are quite minimal, particularly when it came to questions of social and political change. Only rarely among the international security donors do staff or trustees come from the world of social and political activism. So there is a double bind in understanding, much less acting upon, the requirements of social movements. That is one reason why funding experts is easier—the product is palpable (a book, a conference, a study), the mode of activity is uncontroversial, the comfort level with the grantees is higher—than funding social movements. The hurdles to sustained and inventive uses of the energy in something like the freeze, then, are extremely high, particularly in a philanthropic field like international affairs, where the elite and research biases came first and remained sturdy.

The small coterie of donors around David Hunter and Bob Scrivner in the late 1970s did have some ideas about social change, and their funding actions were remarkably timely in promoting both a social movement and the critical communities that aimed to end the arms race. The "strategy" was never detailed or articulated in a comprehensive way; it was almost instinctual, a meeting of different minds and concerns. As more donors entered the field, drawn by both danger and opportunity, this sense of purpose and vision became increasingly accidental or derivative—donors joined in without connecting to the strategic impulses of the original group. The indispensable need for a social movement to change policy, understood intuitively by David Hunter and a few others, seemed not to impress the larger circle of donors involved by 1984. And even the original group did not fully appreciate what they had helped create, did not understand that the power of the freeze, for instance, was its ability to transform attitudes, not its ability to elect politicians or enact arms control. Likewise, few donors understood, even as they were writing grant checks, that the power of the transnational organizations engaging Soviet elites was enabled by Soviet perceptions of the popularity of the arms-reduction proposals in the West. Without this popular upsurge in Western Europe and America, Gorbachev would not have had the political space to undertake the extraordinary risks for disarmament.

The absence of a mechanism for formulating and preserving strategic thinking among donors after those informal lunches of 1979–81 also meant that a learning process was not available to inform philanthropy later on when "institutional memory" was in short supply. There was no place, even in the helpful gatherings of the Forum Institute, where these elements of strategy were debated, distilled, evaluated, and refined. Strategy and tactics were largely improvised all along. The entry of the giants in 1984 skewed much funding toward research and analysis, and away from the movements that created the climate of social-change opportunity that attracted the giants to begin with. So it was easy to forget how the field of activity was originally defined and shaped, and how the policy imperatives of the Reagan administration were revamped to respond to the public outcry of 1980–82. Everything after that was, in a sense, the consolidation of the ground gained by the movement in the early 1980s. What Carnegie, Ford, MacArthur, and Rockefeller were addressing in the mid to late 1980s were questions forcefully raised to the surface of policy urgency by the Traprock Peace Center, Randy Forsberg, the Quakers, Greenpeace, and a thousand other groups, including the freeze. "The *public* discussion of the problems presented by nuclear weaponry which is now taking place in this country is going to go down in history," George Kennan said in 1982, "as the most significant that any democratic society has ever engaged in."[3] Yet by the ratification of the INF Treaty in 1988, this basic lesson, the need for a primal scream of outrage as a precursor to change, was all but forgotten as a deft instrument of philanthropy.

Whether accidental or not, the lesson of the 1980s was quite consistent with how we understand significant policy change takes place. A demand for change emanates from the public, informed by critical thinkers who challenge policy in fundamental ways, and given voice by social movements. Without this combination, little change would have been possible. Critical expertise without social movements is impotent. Experts who are not critical are adjuncts of the state. Social movements without intelligence can be marginalized and ignored. On global issues, the movements and critical communities must be transnational. In confronting the nuclear danger in the 1980s, it all came together.

6

LEAVING THE COLD WAR BEHIND

The end of the Cold War brought with it a sudden sea change in American internationalist philanthropy, as one would expect, and the way it imposed its change was like a hurricane sweeping across a beach front: afterwards, all looks familiar, everything is still there, but a few things are shattered beyond repair and the rest is messily rearranged. The slow-motion implosion of the Soviet empire was like a vacuum at the eye of the storm, but when the Cold War finally ended in 1991, three other forces were afoot, and these were nearly as significant in shaping the philanthropy of the 1990s as the end of the superpower rivalry itself.

The first was the good news emanating in part from the end of the Cold War, but somewhat independent of it: the flourishing of democracy and open societies not only in Eastern Europe, after the sudden retreat of communism in 1989, but in hard cases like South Africa, Chile, and Haiti. The triumph of civil society, of the many nongovernmental organizations spurring these astonishing shifts were on display at the UN conference on sustainability in Rio de Janeiro in 1992—a worldwide explosion of citizen activism that was clearly a force to be reckoned with. The flip side of these revolutions was the fragility of the newly emerging states, economically ruined in many cases, that would require attention from Americans (a topic that I will take up in later chapters).

The second was the crisis occasioned by Iraq's occupation of Kuwait in August 1990, and the war initiated by the U.S.–led alliance five months later. The lead-up to the war encompassed a heady debate about U.S. military intervention and for a time revived the peace movement and split the American public. The debate raised both doubts and hopes about the conduct of a "new world order," and those mixed expectations—about rogue states, nuclear proliferation, arms trafficking, "blood for oil," minorities at risk, and a revitalized United Nations, among others—became features of philanthropy in ensuing years.

After the main phase of the Gulf War was concluded in March 1991, politics in the United States turned to domestic matters, primary among them an economy in recession, with dark foreboding of future gloom. Paul Kennedy's *The Rise and Fall of the Great Powers* (1987) seemed to verify leftists' predilection for bleak scenarios, and the economic downturn, coupled with the Reagan-era cuts in social spending, was distressing. A cry went up for a "peace dividend" to be returned from the flush military budget (I preferred at the time to call it "war reparations" to the American people), and this, too, shaped concerns within the donor community.

All of this was the detritus of the Cold War, the failed states and nuclear wannabes and depleted economies. But they took on a life of their own as reasons to worry, and worry is the root and branch of philanthropy.

For the Winston Foundation, as for many other donors, it was a time to take a look at what we were doing. Our basic support for the grassroots peace movement in this country needed scrutiny, because as a genuine social and political force it was clearly in decline. The professionally based organizations also appeared to be listless. As an emergency measure, we had accepted responsibility for publishing the movement's magazine, *Nuclear Times*, at the end of 1989, and this additional perspective led me to conclude by the summer of 1990 that the fundamental concern driving the movement—the fear of nuclear war—was dissipating rapidly. The temporary surge in antiwar activism during the gulf crisis was just that: temporary, however impressive. (It's easy to forget that 50 percent of the public was wary of, essentially in opposition to, going to war against Iraq.) A disturbing scale of violence was unfolding in Europe, in Yugoslavia, which was earning an infuriating level of official indifference. My own board of directors was restless with what they seemed to consider uninspiring choices of grants. By late 1991 and early 1992, it was quite obvious that we were looking at a very different decade to come. The task for all of us was to identify the sources of trouble we sensed on the horizon and devise plausible funding strategies for dealing with them.

THE GULF WAR AND THE SHAPE OF THINGS TO COME

The most powerful influence of that period was the Gulf War. It raised several troubling questions: the idea of a "resource war," the out-of-control arms trade, a fresh round of confrontation between the West and the Islamic world, and the post-Soviet contours of the nuclear danger. Each of these was daunting and somewhat new to the calculations of donors. Naturally, the nuclear issues—the specter both of rogue states and nuclear proliferation from the former USSR—were core concerns in the arms-control community. The Gulf War and the end of Soviet communism ushered in what I called the "second nuclear age," a period that would be significantly different from the U.S.–Soviet nuclear standoff.

The gulf crisis revealed the grisly dimensions of this period. Its most salient feature was Third World conflict in which the use of chemical or nuclear weapons by combatants was feasible. Many Third World regimes appeared to be on the cusp of owning such weapons by 1990, and some seemed to feel emboldened by the partial breakdown of the global order long imposed by the superpowers. To cope with this situation, a new theory of nuclear deterrence was emerging, and two forms were discernible. The specter of chemical weapons use by Iraq, the possibility of hostage taking, and fears of large numbers of American casualties apparently revived a role for U.S. nuclear arms. The second, and far more plausible, revision of nuclear doctrine was to counter Iraq's nuclear and chemical weapons ambitions with U.S. air strikes against production facilities that manufactured such weaponry.

Nuclear weapons and the doctrines that guided their use had evolved from 1945 almost exclusively in the context of rivalry with the Soviet Union. Although nuclear strikes were contemplated during U.S. wars in Korea and Vietnam, those cases were ad hoc and transitory, though nuclear saber rattling was more common. So the considerations in the gulf were relatively new, at least in the sense that hypothetical situations were giving way to something quite real and harrowing. Saddam Hussein's chemical weapons threats against Israel, made in April 1990, were particularly provocative, and formed the background for the entire gulf crisis.

The first form of the new deterrence—the threat of nuclear reprisal for chemical weapons use or something equally outrageous—was not openly discussed by the U.S. government. But the threat was implicit. American military officials, for example, declared that there would be "no holds barred" in retaliating against Iraqi aggression. And the nuclear firepower was there to do it.[1] The threats became considerably more sobering when the Israeli air force chief-of-staff stated publicly that Israel would retaliate against Iraq with "everything" it had (which included nuclear weapons) should Iraq load their Scud missiles with chemical weapons.

The more plausible form of deterrence was aggressively pursued: the U.S. attack on Iraq's incipient nuclear weapons capability as well as its chemical weapons facilities with air strikes using nonnuclear explosives. The air strikes did not totally cripple Iraq's program, and a long and frustrating UN effort to inspect, monitor, and destroy such capability continued through the decade. What was more disturbing about this episode at the time was the unstated assumption that the legal regimes governing nuclear facilities could not peacefully cope with the problem; a reflexive military response (and essentially illegal under the Nuclear Non-Proliferation Treaty [NPT]) was undertaken instead. Many insisted that Hussein could only be dealt with by force, but they tended to be the same conservatives who had overlooked Reagan's and Bush's prodigious provision to Iraq of financial, political, and intelligence support in the previous decade while Hussein was waging a bloody war against his neighbor Iran. The NPT regime, while quite limited, could not be expected to work when its top cop was dealing goods to the world's premier criminals.

Washington's "new world order" paid such a complaint very little lip service; official thinking, most visible in the 1988 Defense Department study, *Discriminate Deterrence*, instead regarded military action in the Third World as the primary method of coping with post–Cold War concerns. And the Clinton administration followed suit with a "counter-proliferation" strategy that extended this troubling principle of action. NPT would continue to earn support, but the U.S. military would devise options to bomb facilities believed to harbor nuclear and chemical capabilities. One expects such planning from the military; but the embrace by civilian officials, and even the ready endorsement of several proliferation hawks in the arms-control community, was more bothersome. This belligerent view rose to prominence again during the Korea crisis of 1994. But the militant stance on proliferation lingered, despite its ineffectual expression in the bombing of Iraq, and became a staple of a certain segment of the arms-control crowd that continued to earn substantial grants from the peace donors. The reason for this peculiarity lies, I believe, in the origins of the arms-control enterprise itself.

THE CHANGING NATURE OF ARMS CONTROL

The war in the Persian Gulf was waged during the beginnings of the trouble in Yugoslavia, which at first was a bloody skirmish when Croatia seceded and then erupted fully in Bosnia a few weeks after the demise of the Soviet Union. These events demanded fresh scrutiny of the entire arms-control enterprise, which was, after all, a creation of the Cold War, and the Cold War was over.

Examining the salient features of the arms-control process led me to see that it was, in every sense of the term, "technological"—it focused almost exclusively on the technical dimension. Why this was so would tell us much about how to come to grips with the post–Cold War world, a world that seemed to defy the rational, in its sudden embrace of ethnic conflict. One thing seemed certain to me: The nature of arms control—its purpose and form—was being recast in the 1990s. The change derived from a vastly altered political context, even though the technical shape of the weapons deployed was virtually the same.

If one could identify a single, stabilizing factor in the U.S.–Soviet rivalry, it would be this much-maligned arms-control process. A mere cottage industry in the early years of the nuclear age, this process—the research, analysis, diplomacy, military planning, and political management needed to constrain the expansion of nuclear arsenals—grew lavishly from the 1960s until the early 1990s. The growth stemmed from the even more lavish expansion of the weapons this process sought to constrain. (Arms-control studies in universities and think tanks, the entry point into the process for philanthropy, were a primary beneficiary of foundation dollars.) But arms control also flourished because of a unique historical context. The texture of the U.S.–Soviet rivalry proscribed useful dialogue on many central issues—human rights, the Soviet grip on Eastern Europe, and superpower competition in the Third World. It was simply too painful to conduct relations on the basis of "normal" political concerns.

Instead, the nuclear threat became the fulcrum of the *political* relationship. Scientists, lawyers, and specialists in arcane nuclear doctrine came to dominate the deliberations of the two great nations. Negotiating ways to constrain nuclear weapons was regarded by the public as a necessity, above the tussle of propaganda and polemics. The temperature of the relationship was gauged by the vigor of arms-control talks, and misbehavior by either side was often punished by the other's withdrawing from whatever negotiations were then taking place. As the leading edge of the bilateral relationship—and, therefore, of global politics—the arms-control process gained enormous prominence. Its achievements were admirable, even if its failure to halt the arms race was glaring.

The defining feature of arms control, and its ultimate weakness, was its deep devotion to technical matters, namely, the size, scope, and capability of the weapons being controlled. Virtually every aspect was technical, from doctrine to deployment to negotiations to treaty verification. And of course these technical features were its strength, being superior to, or at least separate from, ideology—it was science and engineering, indisputable and immutable. It was precisely this quality that enabled the Pugwash scientists to succeed in bridging the gap to Soviet elites, and accounted for the enormous impact of projects like the seismic verification scheme engineered by the Natural Resources Defense Council (NRDC). People believe scientists to be impartial, above the pettiness of "mere" politics, which is a potent quality. (It also explains why right-wing ideologues so vitriolically sought to slur anti–Star Wars scientists by calling them "flat-Earthers" and the like; the only way to counteract the anti–Star Wars critique was to discredit its technical validity.)

The weakness of arms control appeared in its aversion to normative questions. It was in part this technological fetishism that fueled the right-wing assault on arms control. Reagan undermined the process, however briefly, by challenging its moral premises. What values did it offer? The esoteric formulae of nuclear deterrence appeared to be utterly bereft of moral considerations. What did arms control really offer as a sign of hope in the future if mutually assured destruction remained its pivotal, operational concept? As if to verify this moral bankruptcy, many in the arms-control community declared any longing for weapons cuts to be utopian and offered instead schemes for better command-and-control of the nuclear weapons, yet another technical approach that many found to be the last breath of a brain-dead weapons elite (much of it also supported by American philanthropy).

Solutions to the nuclear deadlock that were more intentionally political—the nuclear freeze, the comprehensive nuclear test ban, and the nonoffensive defense—were dismissed by many arms controllers as displaying insufficient technical rigor. When Gorbachev turned all equations on their head by embracing a new politics of disarmament, one that had a scientific grounding but made leaps beyond where traditional arms controllers were willing to go, the "radical" ideas of the test ban, the zero option, and so forth suddenly had cachet and the technical details were nearly forgotten. Gorbachev reintroduced the importance of the political relationship, the actual intentions of the adversary, as the key variable. And, ever since, the threat of intentional nuclear war between Russia and the United States has seemed all the more like an absurdity, despite the fact that the size of the nuclear deployments remained excessive and potentially as devastating as ever. (The technological emphasis could and was turned on arms-control advocates in the 1990s when the test ban, negotiated for decades and signed in 1996, was defeated in the U.S. Senate in 1999 ostensibly on technical grounds.)

The cult of the technical—of legalisms and treaties and verification schemes—persisted beyond the demise of the USSR and began to center in the 1990s on "rogue" states (Iran, Iraq, North Korea, and Libya), proliferation via the former Soviet Union, and some specific trouble spots, such as the India-Pakistan confrontation. None of the viable solutions to these potential emergencies are mainly technical in character. Each involves diplomacy to induce the misbehaving to behave. Convincing a Ukraine or Kazakhstan to forego a nuclear capability, as the Clinton administration did successfully in 1993–94, has more to do with political and economic enticements than with nuclear doctrine. A more urgent example in that same period was the effort to blunt North Korea's nuclear weapons program, a political agreement that set out certain incentives and sanctions. The crisis over North Korea in 1994 came close to becoming a very nasty war, and was defused by President Clinton's wisely stepping back from the precipice. There was ample pressure to hit North Korean nuclear sites—some of the pressure again being mounted by an arms-control community obsessed with North Korea's purported nuclear program—an action that very likely would have started a major war. It is noteworthy that the North Korean agreement was partly the result of a private initiative, involving, among others, Jimmy Carter, and mainly funded with innovative flair by Tom Graham of the Rockefeller Foundation. At root, it was a political agreement, something that continues to earn the enmity of those who like to dwell on the technical "loopholes." But it worked throughout the remainder of the decade, despite tremendous flux in North Korea.

The India-Pakistan confrontation illustrates the same point. The nuclear weapons capability of each, confirmed in their series of nuclear tests in May 1998, has long been a focal point of international security specialists. The nuclear tests stirred U.S. officials to redouble efforts to coerce India and Pakistan to sign nuclear-control treaties. News coverage of the events fastened on the potential for nuclear catastrophe, the possible numbers of warheads and delivery systems, and the scientists behind the tests. But the India-Pakistan rivalry was not about nuclear weapons. The source of trouble goes back hundreds of years to the invasion by and migration of Muslims into Hindu India, and, more recently, the bloody partition of India in 1947, when British rule ended and an Islamic state of Pakistan was sliced out of India. One million people were killed in communal violence in the late 1940s. That kind of pain and enmity does not dissipate in two or three generations.

Matters of prestige and respect also exert weight on India's nuclear decision making. In 1971, President Nixon sent the *U.S.S. Enterprise*, a nuclear-capable aircraft carrier, into the Bay of Bengal during the India-Pakistan war. The war began when Pakistan brutally suppressed an autonomy movement in East Pakistan (now Bangladesh), sending thousands of refugees into India, which moved to support the Bengalis. In a foolish bit of gunboat diplomacy, Nixon ordered the *Enterprise* to sail toward the Indian coast, implicitly threatening the New Delhi government. As Peter Clausen wrote in his classic analytical work, *Nonproliferation and the National Interest*, "the *Enterprise* episode was an affront to Indian national pride that left a lasting imprint on the country's security thinking. These factors reinforced the momentum of India's nuclear program." Shortly after that, in 1974, Prime Minister Indira Gandhi ordered India's first nuclear test. The Indians and to a lesser extent the Pakistanis have also argued for decades that NPT is discriminatory by allowing those countries with nuclear weapons (then the United States, Britain, France, China, and the USSR) in effect to retain them, while prohibiting acquisition by others. While the treaty obligated the five nuclear powers to disarm, that obligation was significantly ignored. "We don't want to be blackmailed and treated as oriental blackies," a spokesman for the nationalist Bharatiya Janata Party, now in power, said several years before the nuclear tests. "Nuclear weapons will give us prestige, power, standing. An Indian will talk straight and walk straight when we have the bomb."[2] That signals a set of political problems—not technical or legal—which coercion to sign this or that agreement will not solve.

The bloody manifestation of this conflict today is the war in the Himalayan province of Kashmir, nominally under the control of India but where Muslims outnumber Hindus and where both states claimed sovereignty. Clinton aides in the wake of the atomic blasts suddenly saw Kashmir as something to which they should pay more attention. In fact, it's festered for decades. The political and psychological wounds of so many years are the reason why India and Pakistan developed nuclear weapons. Nukes are a symptom, not the disease. But the arms-control process treats the arms problem as the disease, a simple matter of injecting some logic and legalisms. It is an approach that will ensure that an outbreak will return again and again.

The concerns over nuclear rogues in the early 1990s were accentuated by a new awareness of conventional arms proliferation, a topic previously ignored by public interest groups and earning the interest of only a very few analysts. Hussein's ability to construct such a formidable military by importing virtually everything brought the issue home, and even the Bush administration promised to do something about the arms trade (which, of course, they did not). The hope to stem arms trafficking was long overshadowed by nuclear issues—and earned some attention from donors mainly because some of the trade was in missiles that could deliver nuclear weapons—and often was shoehorned into the nuclear arms-control mold. The problem, which earned a fleeting spotlight in the mid-1970s when Nixon and Kissinger were selling everything imaginable to the Shah of Iran and other dictators, was addressed briefly during the Carter administration in a negotiation with the Soviet Union, a bumbled attempt hindered by breathtaking naïveté, and of course it failed miserably. The variety of conventional weapons, the multiplicity of manufacturers, and the ubiquity of the weapons all argued for a fresh approach, one that again eschewed the technical for the political. Gradually, over time, the disarmament community in Washington adopted more nuanced strategies, mainly beholden to the human rights model of action—monitoring violations and embarrassing perpetrators.

By the end of the decade, the altered context of arms control was apparent. Even the great nuclear rivalry between Russia and America was stuck on very *un*technical political quarrels: the xenophobia and resurgent nationalism of right-wing deputies in the Russian Duma who held the second Strategic Arms Reduction Treaty (START II) hostage, the growing corruption throughout Russia, and the religio-ethnic conflicts in Chechnya, Bosnia, and Kosovo. The NPT was weakened by the endless imbroglio in Iraq, the North Korean instability, and the Indian and Pakistani nuclear explosions. The nuclear test ban treaty was defeated by the xenophobes in the U.S. Senate (principally to embarrass Clinton), and the Anti-Ballistic Missile Treaty was under pressure from those (the same xenophobes, plus defense contractors) still clinging to dreams of a missile defense. It was a sorry state of affairs for the great and noble enterprise of arms control, an undeserved fate, and avoidable with more political courage here and there. Certainly the philanthropic community exerted itself maximally to keep it viable. But its fate was not altogether surprising, given its origins in the U.S.–Soviet confrontation. Once that was finished, everything else would change.

DISMANTLING THE NATIONAL SECURITY STATE

The infamous military-industrial complex, long an archnemesis of liberal donors, was another artifact of the Cold War that seemed impervious to reform. An especially sore point was the military economy—excessive Pentagon spending, the dependency of many sectors of the economy on military research and development and procurement, and the sense that the military was crowding out other federal priorities. This set of complaints went back at least to the Vietnam

War period, and in fact Vietnam was one of the reasons 1980s activists insisted on cutting the military budget. President Johnson's unwillingness to raise taxes to pay for the war was widely viewed as a cause of the growing federal budget deficits and price inflation that buffeted the American economy in the 1970s. As the war was winding down, too, the technical superstructure that grew in the 1960s—the scientists and engineers designing weapons—was suddenly shrunk, throwing thousands out of work. Seymour Melman's landmark 1974 study, *The Permanent War Economy*, argued persuasively that the military-industrial complex was bad for the economy, breeding inefficiency and secrecy while soaking up precious resources.

Dozens of organizations sprang up to oppose the expanding Reagan budgets and still more were created to convert military factories and bases to civilian uses. Virtually every funder in the nuclear field also made grants on the defense budget. It was not merely the waste that drove these dollars into this endeavor, it was the sense that the costs of the Cold War might be regarded by the public as an intolerable burden. For people already prone to suspect all things military, the economic arguments—always assumed to appeal more to the average American than the arcana of nuclear doctrine—seemed like a surefire way to strike a blow for peace.

At the root of this belief was the plausible idea that presidents, generals, and admirals, flush with more soldiers and weaponry, would be keener to engage in Third World intervention or even something riskier. That a large and growing military is more prone to mischief seemed obvious: The end of the Vietnam War, after all, was only five years before Reagan was elected. Reagan himself was gradually committing to military intervention in Central America, deploying Marines (disastrously) in Lebanon, and invading Grenada. In military circles there was incessant talk about "force projection" and "low-intensity conflict." And the aggressive procurement of new strategic nuclear weapons seemed to accelerate arms racing with the Soviet Union.

The second reason to attack Pentagon spending was its effect on the U.S. economy. During Reagan's presidency, defense outlays equaled 6.6 percent of all national economic output, the highest since the 1950s and far higher than the comparable spending by economic rivals like West Germany and Japan. As Melman had pointed out a decade earlier, this system of large expenditures and bureaucratic management soaked up capital, scientific talent, and productive capacity, and was creating no consumer goods in return—a bad economic bargain. It appeared to sacrifice social policy, too: the high budgets drove up the federal deficit and interest rates, and squeezed the government funds available for social service programs. (Reagan's budget chief later admitted this outcome was intentional.) The Pentagon itself was exceptionally adept at building political support for unnecessary and costly weapons; the B-1 bomber, it was widely noted, had procurement contracts in every congressional district. Defense jobs were unionized and high paying, and as other federal spending shriveled in the Reagan era and industrial unemployment grew, these jobs were fiercely protected by Congress. All of these practices added up to a system of grotesque excess—not only wasteful, but dangerous.

The peace movement and a sizable number of economists and business leaders pressed the arguments for reducing the burden of Pentagon profligacy. Opinion makers, while hardly unanimous, also questioned the size of the Reagan budgets, especially in light of the Vietnam-era experience and America's painful economic performance since the late 1960s. These efforts clearly impressed the public and Congress, which struggled with Reagan over the budgets.

By the time the Cold War was clearly in decline, the Bush administration acted fairly quickly to reduce the defense burden. The dollar peak was in 1990, after which significant cuts of nearly 25 percent were pursued. Though far short of the "peace dividend" many clamored for, the decline in military spending came at a time of economic doldrums. Given the enormous clout of the defense lobby—which includes all aerospace manufacturers, much of the electronics industry, and the major labor unions—the drop in military budgets when the economy seemed to need the stimulus of greater spending is particularly notable. And the momentum for reducing the military burden lasted well into the 1990s. By the end of President Clinton's first term in 1997 (and after two years of a Republican Congress that arrested the decline in military spending), the Pentagon's share of national output dropped in half from the Reagan peak, down to about 3.3 percent. Procurement of new weapons and equipment was half of the 1990 purchases, and one-third of 1985 purchases. As a share of the federal budget, the military was at 15.5 percent in fiscal 1998 compared with 28 percent in 1987. In inflation-adjusted dollars, 50 percent more was spent on defense at its last peak in 1989. Granted, all of this is in comparison with the bloat of the Reagan period. But the trends were clearly downward, even though traditional pressures for spending—the defense lobby, resurgent conservatives, and the like—were strong.

The efforts to "convert" the thousands of defense facilities to civilian use was more mixed. Defense bases, which are federal property and can be easily transformed to other uses (parks and recreation, housing, airports, industrial sites, and so on), were gradually closed and converted, though this, too, ran into congressional opposition. The local campaigns to convert defense firms to commercial production, however, almost entirely failed. The sharp contrast between these two related attempts at conversion can be explained by how the decisions are made. The fate of the military bases was and is decided by Congress (recommended by a base-closure commission), a somewhat transparent, publicly accountable process. Decisions about the fate of defense-production firms are made privately, by corporate management. While the Pentagon had influence over these firms, many of which were almost completely dependent on defense contracts, they were essentially beyond the reach of public wishes. Many defense firms did move toward commercial production, though their answer to lower defense spending also involved significant layoffs, mergers with other defense firms to protect their share of Pentagon contracts, and energetic bids to export weaponry abroad.

By the mid-1990s, when it suddenly appeared that the decline in defense spending may have been temporary and the defense budget still had Cold War proportions—nearly $300 billion, more than the combined budgets of the next eight military "powers," including China, Russia, and Iran—a number of advocacy organizations wanted to mount a new campaign to reduce Pentagon spending. With the notable exception of Ben Cohen, of Ben & Jerry's fame, few donors bought in. The reasons for this reluctance to reengage this issue are complex. For the Winston Foundation, which carefully considered the military economy as a possible emphasis when we reassessed our grant making in 1992, the reason boiled down to one issue: It was simply not compelling enough when compared with other needs.

The two major criticisms underlying the critique of Pentagon spending in the 1970s and 1980s—overfeeding a frisky military, and damaging the economy—no longer described the cardinal reasons to constrain Pentagon spending in the 1990s. The arena of concern remains both the uses and misuses of the military, and the American economy. But the complexion of each had already changed by the time the Cold War ended.

The U.S. military, while still flush with weapons and soldiers, is an immense bureaucracy and thereby an innately cautious institution. Its taste for military intervention is meager, and in the post-Vietnam period it has been virtually nonexistent. Colin Powell's Hamlet-like hesitancy about the use of force is now official doctrine. The tardy response to genocide in Bosnia was a stark example of the reigning spirit of the new military. And with the disappearance of the USSR, the notion of an arms race does not carry the same meaning as it did fifteen or twenty years ago.

The Pentagon's bearing on the economy also differs from recent decades. Among the effects of this lower share of national output are the salutary benefits for price inflation: the Pentagon is no longer as big a competitor for raw materials or workers; nor does it pump so many wages into the economy. These effects are bound to have a measurable, happy influence on prices, though economists are divided on this matter. That the U.S. economy expanded in the 1990s with low inflation from about the time the Pentagon budget began to shrink cannot be merely coincidental. Nor is the wild expansion of high-tech industries once the talent was attracted to the sexy electronics firms of Silicon Valley rather than the high-paying, self-important military research empires. The military simply does not have the impact—for good or ill—on economic activity that it once did.

So military spending as a pivot point of a funding program seemed much less compelling in 1992 than it did a decade earlier. And in 1992–93, with the onset of the Clinton presidency, the promise of a more restrained spending agenda looked solid. Clinton even proposed a conversion program to be housed in the Pentagon. Had we known then that many of these ideas would never get traction, and that the military's downward trend of spending would be reversed in the late 1990s, it would not have affected our decision to forego a major campaign against Pentagon budgets. The critical communities had simply lost their rigor. They could no longer articulate reasons why such spending posed the societal or security threat it once represented; the critique rested mainly on wastefulness, a regrettable fact but hardly the first federal program to be so encumbered. And there was very little public outrage about high military budgets apparent, even in the recession of the 1990s. Defense firms offered some of the only good jobs in a period of "de-industrialization," and this seemed to overwhelm scattered concerns about Pentagon waste.

At a peace donors meeting in Washington in early 1992, the confusion of the time was underscored by a poll commissioned by the Ottinger Foundation. The pollster, Stan Greenberg, who was also polling for Bill Clinton's campaign, had asked a sizable sample of respondents about cutting spending, and what concerned them in the post–Cold War world. The results, Greenberg told the gathering, were not wholly satisfying. The public was not keen to cut spending more than the 25 percent being promised at the time. And one of the reasons they were reluctant to cut more was because the world still appeared to be a dangerous place, made so by threats like nuclear proliferation. I remarked afterwards that as a donor community we were promoting deep cuts in defense at the same time we were scaring the public with noisy alarms about loose nukes and rogue states: It didn't add up, and the public knew it.

of the Peace Development Fund. A number of old arms-control groups even tried to refurbish themselves to fit the ecological fashions, designing programs that wove together security and environmentalism.

"Foundations love movements when they're hot," says Pablo Eisenberg, the longtime director of the Center for Community Change. "Usually, they won't fund social-change organizations." When the freeze declined and the movement looked like it was going downhill, the old habits returned. As noted earlier, a number of donors did not consider their investments in the grassroots movements and advocacy think tanks as having paid the dividends they foresaw, and Reagan's participation in dismantling the Cold War robbed many liberals of any sense of satisfaction.

For those who remained (and most of the original set did remain), the strategy for peace in the world would take many forms. Not among them was the sustaining of a popular movement in the United States to make public demands for peace—for new federal priorities, for an end to dealing weapons, for preventive diplomacy, for total nuclear disarmament. The great social movements for peace of the 1980s were quickly waning by the end of the Reagan presidency. An ample reservoir of interest and organizing skill remained in place, but the scale was altogether different. The nuclear danger had vanished as a *personal* concern for the educated, middle-class core of the peace movement. The dissolution of the nuclear threat happened so quickly and unexpectedly that there was little time to adjust to the new era. Could a sizable social movement be mobilized around issues of the arms trade or loose nukes or the failure to pay UN dues? Apparently not. The lethargy soon became visible in falling membership and organizing vigor. After the brief resurgence of opposition to the Gulf War, the grassroots peace movement was a pale imitation of its recently former self—no one's fault, really, and not surprising, given its successes. But for donors who recognized the value of popular agitation, for things like pressure on politicians from their home precincts, the demise of the movement was not a pretty sight. "The lack of grassroots activism in the '90s was not due to a lack of interest by funders," says George Perkovich of the W. Alton Jones Foundation. "Funders would support the grassroots if there were credible groups out there." That sentiment was echoed by Marty Teitel of the C. S. Fund, an early supporter of Randy Forsberg: "We saw this fantastic drop-off in what we consider to be fundable proposals."[2] The unanswerable chicken-and-egg question is whether the funders abandoned the grassroots movement prematurely, consigning it to its decline, or if funders saw the obvious signs of decline and opted to invest elsewhere. Some theories of social change insist that if the resources can be mobilized—and money is the mother lode of resources—then the movements will appear. The decline of peace activism would pose a stiff challenge to that theory.

DONORS RECKON WITH THE NEW WORLD ORDER

"When you've been working for fifteen years on a single subject, a big, complex subject, and it completely turns inside-out, how do you keep your bearings?" That sentiment, expressed by a research colleague, encapsulates the bizarre challenge of change confronting the peace movement, arms-control intellectuals, and the donors at the end of 1991, when the Soviet Union dissolved. For at least a decade, the peace donors had worked in the context of the Cold War, and while it was clearly being disassembled from about 1987 onward, its rapid collapse following the Communist *putsch* of August 1991 was still a surprise.

"By 1990, we were thinking about the post–Cold War era," recalls Ruth Adams, then head of MacArthur's program. "There was great euphoria, a sense we could all start afresh, and there were great problems, too—authoritarian leaders, refugees, and crippled economies. Our staff people were thinking about this and wrote many wonderful papers about human rights, civil society, and so on, very visionary. It was a wonderful experiment." The themes at MacArthur were demilitarization, defense conversion, the role of the military in society, the reconstruction tasks after the Cold War, how to create a new world order, and what the American role would and should be.

"We took the metaphor of the war, the end of the war, quite seriously," says Kennette Benedict, who was Adams's deputy then and runs the program now. "We started with some sketchy ideas and developed a grant-making strategy for each of them" in what became a four-point program: arms control and disarmament, sustainable democracy (including a "Marshall Plan" for the former USSR), international governance and civil society, and U.S. interests and priorities. "We met with a lot of outsiders," Benedict notes, "and by early '91 we were ready to take the new program to the board." The relatively conservative MacArthur board of the early 1980s (which included radio commentator Paul Harvey) had gradually become more progressive and knowledgeable, and to some degree the grants reflected that. A major initiative to normalize relations with Cuba was undertaken. Exploring the meaning of the end of the Cold War was supported by several grants, including those to the leftish Institute for Policy Studies and the Center for National Security Studies, which was to consider "ending the Cold War at home." The Peace Development Fund got a half million dollars to support a strategy of defense conversion. And the Helsinki Citizens Assembly, an effort to build civil society through-out Europe, received an organization-building grant of $300,000.

The MacArthur emphasis on the domestic issues—"A lot of people never thought about the impact of the Cold War on the U.S.," Ruth Adams explains—was a common theme among donors in the 1989–92 period. Among others, Ploughshares, Winston, Rubin, the John Merck Fund, and Wade Greene's group of Rockefeller donors contributed to the effort to extract a "peace dividend." But the larger concern was about Russia. MacArthur created an innovative approach by launching a foundation-wide program in the former Soviet Union that addressed multiple concerns—energy, environment, women, human rights, and denuclearization. The Rockefeller Brothers Fund pursued an assertive program of building civil society in Eastern Europe. The Carnegie Corporation invested in a program at the Kennedy School called Strengthening Democratic Institutions, which, in the words of Carnegie president David Hamburg, "has been a dynamic and valuable source of practical advice for those concerned with building democratic institutions."[3] They backed that up with millions of dollars in grants to Harvard University over the next few years.

During the Gulf War, Hamburg declared his interest in developing a system to constrain the arms trade, a multilateral force to intervene where arms buildups were menacing, and regional legal mechanisms. While none of those notions came to fruition, each one reflected the surge of interest in conventional arms restraint just then, and Carnegie's intentions were not the only ones to fall on hard times. An ambitious idea to build a global, early warning network of researchers, called Arms Watch, was developed by the Rockefeller Foundation, only to be scuttled at the last minute by its president Peter Goldmark, who apparently had cold feet; he instead unloaded about a million dollars a year on Human Rights Watch to watch arms the way it monitored human rights violations.

"I think foundations floundered at the end of the Cold War," observes John Redick, who by 1991 was no longer at W. Alton Jones, but continued to consult to some donors. "They did not seize the opportunity to make a major change away from high military spending, did not try to strengthen the UN or regional organizations, or educate the public about international engagement. Instead I saw trustees walk away and look for a new fad. The end of the Cold War was the end of excitement. It was a time for maturity from foundations, and that did not happen. I would put W. Alton Jones in that category."

Certainly, the overall trajectory of funding did not seem to change dramatically from the mid-1980s, when the giants entered, to the mid-1990s, when the euphoria of the Cold War's demise had worn off. The giants were funding the kinds of organizations they always had, for the most part, with some notable variations according to the acquisition of new themes. Carnegie's long-standing attachment to Harvard's Kennedy School, for example, began with nuclear management techniques and morphed into democratic advice-giving. The balance between support for social movements and elite-oriented groups gravitated toward the latter in part because the grassroots movement was by 1992 in a shakeout that would reduce its scope and numbers by about 80 percent from its peak. As Barbara Dudley, the Veatch Program head at the time, asks rhetorically, "Can you really blame funders for not supporting a movement that was falling apart?"

But the trend away from funding local organizations, or the large membership organizations, was done mainly with a lament and shrug of the shoulders rather than as a widely deliberated strategy. What were the consequences of placing all the bets on scholars or the Washington-based advocacy groups and think tanks? Were other social movement strategies possible? The Gulf War had a major impact on funders' sense of the new dangers in the world, especially weapons proliferation, but it not seem to affect thinking about how the U.S. government was shaping its policies. The war, said HKH Foundation head Harriet Barlow at the time, "lays to rest the illusion that it is possible to achieve these things without dealing with the issue of power."[4]

Not a great deal of thought worked over those kinds of questions, at least not as a collective discussion among donors. The donors simply did not come together in a consistently collaborative way. Critical communities continued to gain support, but the link between new, challenging ideas in security and the pressure from below necessary to rattle policy makers was no longer strong and vital. And that weak link was most noticeable in the field of work where the link was once strongest: in addressing the nuclear danger.

THE NUCLEAR NINETIES

For most peace donors, the remnant of commonality in the decade after the Cold War was concern about nuclear proliferation. A number of sophisticated organizations run by mature experts were at the head of this class—the Carnegie Endowment for International Peace, Nuclear Control Institute, Wisconsin Project for Nuclear Arms Control, and Monterrey Institute, among a few others. The instantaneous menace of loose nukes from the former USSR made these groups the natural inheritors of the fight against the nuclear danger. Prominent in their continuing commitment to arms control were all of the Rockefeller philanthropies except the Rockefeller Family Fund, plus Ford, Carnegie, and MacArthur, the Ploughshares Fund, the John Merck Fund, Prospect Hill Foundation, and a few others, including Winston. Oddly, the primary donor in this field, the Rockefeller Brothers Fund (RBF), under the tenacious program direction of Hilary Palmer, decided to abandon it at the exact moment when its salience was highest. Their leading role eventually came under the exceptionally capable guidance of George Perkovich of the W. Alton Jones Foundation. But the exit of RBF from the field, apparently done to make room for other interests of its president, looked much like the nightmare-come-true of many activists and researchers—that foundation decisions are capricious and illogical. "There was never a full board discussion about phasing out the program," notes someone close to process.

Among all the donors involved, the nonproliferation enterprise possibly enjoyed a fuller degree of consensus than nuclear issues had a decade earlier. Efforts on behalf of stopping the spread of nuclear technologies and materials tended toward a rather modest goal: renewal of the Nuclear Non-Proliferation Treaty (NPT). This goal was attained in 1995, and it was not a small achievement. At root, however, NPT's extension was due to the desire of the major powers, mainly the nuclear club itself, to keep this sole nonproliferation mechanism intact. Advocacy work on export controls (halting American export of technologies that could help in a nuclear weapons program) and stopping the production of plutonium, a key ingredient in most nuclear weapons, yielded more disappointing results. The plutonium ban, in fact, was meant to be the next great nonproliferation measure following NPT and the nuclear test ban, but it never got traction.

The spotty record on nuclear nonproliferation was matched by the organizations promoting nuclear abolition—reductions far more radical than what was envisioned in the strategic arms reduction talks process. At one point, more than a dozen different studies pushing for abolition were under way. They failed to resonate in part because the Russians were no longer interested in disarmament, seeing nuclear weapons as a vestige of superpower prestige. This attitude was not easily amenable to American philanthropy's strategy for the old Soviet arsenal: The overwhelming amount of foundation money for dealing with the Russian problem went to experts, here and in Moscow. But a dearth of expertise was not the problem; rather, the dearth of political will was the main obstacle to Russian cooperation.

On virtually all of the nuclear issues, the absence of a serious social movement was telling. This absence was not only true for the initiatives that never had a popular profile, such as the plutonium ban, but was also evident in the case of the matters of long-standing public involvement. President Bush's go-slow approach to the strategic arms reduction talks—specifically, his in-depth review of U.S.–Soviet relations in 1989—was a lethal delay of the momentum created by his predecessor and patron, and this irresponsible dawdling sparked no public outcry because of the perception of lowered nuclear danger. The test ban is an even more obvious example. Three episodes should have convinced us that progress on these still-difficult issues was unlikely without a popular outcry. When in 1994 a trial balloon was sent up by the White House hinting of new nuclear tests, it stirred a sharp response from NGOs, led in Washington by Daniel Ellsberg, who was then running the small, antinuclear Manhattan II Project, and taken up by the residual grassroots activists. Clinton immediately backed down and signed a test ban agreement in 1996. The French nuclear tests in the Pacific also prompted an enormous, worldwide protest, led by networks of groups in the region, which muscled the French to agree to no more testing. The third example is the obverse: the defeat of the test ban accord by the Senate in October 1999. In this, the heads-in-the-sand Republicans were to blame, apparently punishing Clinton for his sexual misdeeds. In the absence of a vociferous, broad-based public campaign to ratify the treaty, it was left to stand alone, vulnerable to the irresponsible pettiness of the Republican leadership.

"So many people think the nuclear problem is solved," says George Perkovich. "There's an amazement at the idea that people still work on it. So the grassroots can't be expected to be mobilized." While overall numbers of foundations giving to arms-control issues did sink sharply, from more than 75 in 1984 to 55 in 1988 to 25 in 1994, the dollar amounts from foundations were not as dramatically in decline. Contributions from individuals—especially through direct mail campaigns—dropped much more precipitously. But what the falloff in numbers did mean was that the better-heeled were seeking money from the large foundations, which induced a self-perpetuating cycle of elite-oriented work. It meant there was less diversity in the field. Perhaps that is why the self-assessments of success are so modest. "One of our disappointments was the Coalition Against the Nuclear Danger," says MacArthur's Kennette Benedict, citing one of the major coalitions of nuclear arms-control groups in the 1990s. "It takes more than smart people and well-organized programs to get things done." Perkovich, who authored a major history of India's nuclear program, concurs: "It's a strategy that's not working," although he points with justifiable pride to the Nunn-Lugar legislation to help Russian scientists, back-channel meetings on Middle East security, and some track two diplomacy between India and Pakistan. Similarly, Hilary Palmer's tenure at the Rockefeller Brothers

Fund was focused on the NPT extension as its major monument. None of these achievements are trivial. But they do underscore the limits of high-level advocacy in absence of a public demand. By the end of the decade, the nuclear test ban was defeated in the U.S. Senate, Russia continued to block the second Strategic Arms Reduction Treaty (START II), India and Pakistan were openly nuclear powers, ballistic missile defense was declared official administration policy, and the NPT itself was under constant barrage from Iraq, North Korea, Israel, and others. This outcome did not warm the heart of an arms-control funder.

GATHERING THE ELITES

Bereft of a discernable emphasis on social change, philanthropy in the early to mid-1990s evinced a new faith in elites. Colossal amounts of money were poured into gold-plated commissions to study the challenges of the post–Cold War world. Often the same names appeared on these panels, which were fashioned after the relatively successful Palme and Brandt commissions. These many blue-ribbon committees drew familiar conclusions: America should devote more money to foreign aid; pay its dues to the United Nations and be more cooperative generally with multilateral security agencies; strengthen ties to Europe (or Africa, Latin America, Asia, the Middle East, et cetera); uphold standards of human rights, women's equality, ecological sustainability, market-based economies, and the rule-of-law; pursue and protect legitimate national interests (never clearly defined); and abolish nuclear weapons.

There was nothing wrong with the ideas proffered by this veritable posse of policy mavens. They were sensible and at times insightful. They matched up well against the right wing's version of grand strategy, which called for more military spending, more aggressive nuclear doctrine, less foreign aid, market-based economies, and unilateral American action to protect national interests (never clearly defined). But the more liberal policy-shaping efforts failed to do something very fundamental to their purported goal to redirect foreign policy: engage the American public in a sustained and aggressive way.

The lure of the commission is not difficult to understand. The device was among the more successful foundation ventures in the 1960s, when those convened by Ford, Carnegie, and others studied problems and recommended reforms that were often taken to heart by decision makers in Washington, Albany, Sacramento, and elsewhere. Among the most glittering of these was Ford's excursion into public television—an early, pioneering foray by McGeorge Bundy—which resulted in the Public Broadcasting System, and Carnegie's Commission on Educational Television and the Carnegie Commission on Higher Education, which, in the words of one observer, "in breadth of coverage, quality, objectivity, and impact on public policy the work . . . constituted probably the most important body of descriptive and analytical literature about American higher education ever produced"[5] as did a number of other commissions that were chaired by former leaders—the Brandt Commission, the Bruntdland Commission, and others. A similar set of activities, on a smaller scale, were the meetings of scientists who conducted "summer studies" of particular problems of security, often with considerable impact. The era of these elite teams had passed by the 1990s, however. The novelty of the commissions of the 1960s was one of their most powerful attributes. Within a couple of decades, such uniqueness or relevance had dissipated.

Despite the shrinking prospect of affecting history on the strength of a glossy report, the decade after the Berlin Wall fell witnessed the rise of dozens of commissions, high-level studies, and task forces purporting to redefine security. Virtually all were made possible by lavish support from the large American foundations. They gathered many of the same people, and chose names that blur in recollection: International Peace and Security in a New World System, Cooperative Security Project, Commission on Global Governance, Rethinking America's Security, National Commission on America and the New World, The Commission on America's National Interests, America's Task in a Changing World, and so on. These conclaves, typically drawing on scholars or former policy makers whose opinions were already in print, were drawn out affairs requiring immense expenditures for the first-class handling of the participants. (Altogether, the total must reach well into the tens, possibly even hundreds, of millions of dollars.) The conclusions were rarely groundbreaking; the ground had been tilled on the favorite concept—common or cooperative security—fifteen or twenty years earlier by peace researchers in Europe. "I would present a paper based on something I'd written two or three years earlier," a frequent participant explains. "The purpose for going was to be there, to be among those who might be important to one's future some day, or to see old friends, or to enjoy the mountain air."

All these efforts purported to redefine security, but none achieved anything so lofty. "Scores of competing paradigms or quasi-paradigms appeared on the scene, none capable of capturing the imagination or support of either scholars or policymakers to say nothing of the public at large," wrote Stephen Del Rosso, then a program officer at the Pew Charitable Trusts. "An additive 'laundry list' approach to security became commonplace; a series of emerging (or more evident) threats—from drug trafficking to global warming—were appended to a steadily increasing inventory that was once primarily limited to military concerns. The cumulative product, largely devoid of any coherent, overarching framework, became the basis for a raft of dimly remembered and rarely consulted academic and 'policy-relevant' pieces that, for the most part, gathered dust on library shelves."[6]

The outcome of these commissions or summer institutes was typically a book, a report, a series of papers, and, of course, more conferences. The self-published works have virtually no durable value. The claim that the networking among the high-level conferees was a benefit is plausible, but difficult to justify the costs, given the ample opportunities they have to work together. Equally spurious is the hope that some participants would be selected for high office and then implement the new vision of the commission; that was dispelled by the few who did in fact make it into decision-making posts. That these many talkfests have passed unnoticed into the mists of think tank history should come as no surprise. They had no concept of how a new idea could reshape national or global security practices apart from a vague reliance on elitism. The apparent assumption was simply that elites still ruled, and the more elites one could marshal, the more likely some satisfying outcome would materialize.

In a country where "redefining global security" was as low a public priority as one could imagine, the possibility of moving decision makers with the power of a book that said much the same as three dozen other, already-ignored volumes, was rather small. The convenors of the commissions (sometime the foundation officers themselves) failed to learn from the 1980s, in particular, when a number of studies of complex security issues altered the contours of foreign policy discourse and decisions. In these instances—the nuclear freeze proposal itself (which, among other places, was published in *Scientific American*) and the opposition to Star Wars come readily to mind—the people involved framed the subject in ways that were salient to the public, and then purposefully set out to mobilize the public to make these ideas salient to decision makers. That required organizations capable of such involvement with the public, of course. The nuclear freeze activists, the Union of Concerned Scientists (UCS) or the Federation of American Scientists, among others, were repeatedly able to articulate complex, even arcane, ideas and then rouse the interested public enough to impress Congress and the White House. One could argue that they were in the midst of a red-hot national controversy, and that mobilizing the public was relatively easy. But they did so on extraordinarily small budgets (UCS's budget for that activity in the mid-1980s was less than one million dollars, including their "blue ribbon" reports). The commissions of the 1990s had no connection to ordinary concerns or politics. So, not able or willing to fertilize change with their exertions, they appeared in the end to be no more than mere self-gratification.

The embarrassing record with commissions exposes three tendencies that are endemic to a large swath of philanthropy. First is a class bias that consistently favors the professionals, the universities, and the research centers over the great unwashed of a "people's movement" like Acorn or Peace Action and even progressive labor unions. Second is the absence of an operating conception of how policy change actually occurs. Ideas about *what* should happen were always abundant. But ideas about *how* things actually happen were in short supply. It is an unexamined habit of philanthropy that reverberates, year after year, through all its giving. Third is the risk aversion of those in charge—the inability to accept a high rate of failure in selecting projects to support in the expectation that a few gems will be unearthed.

THE ROAD TO DAMASCUS GOES THROUGH SARAJEVO

Making effective choices about how to manifest good policy ideas was complicated by a new opportunity for elite-driven change that appeared soon after the U.S.–Soviet rivalry ended: the onset of the Clinton presidency. The critical communities remaining were faced with the unusual prospect of becoming part of a governing elite, with the administration absorbing dozens of people once among the arms-control and disarmament communities. Mort Halperin, John Shattuck, Frank von Hippel, Larry Smith, Gloria Duffy, and Lee Feinstein, among the many others who populated the advocacy groups of the liberal NGO community, were asked into the Defense Department, the State Department, or the White House staff. Anthony Lake, a longtime friend of the peace community, was appointed Clinton's national security adviser. Hazel O'Leary, who as secretary of energy had oversight of the weapons labs and nuclear production complex, brought in Dan Richter of NRDC and Bob Alvarez of the Friends of the Earth. Joseph Nye and Graham Allison of the Kennedy School "owls" came in at high levels. Rob Stein became chief-of-staff of the Commerce Department under Ron Brown. The shift of people around the imperial city also had an impact on Capitol Hill: Les Aspin's move to become secretary of defense, for example, meant that longtime Pentagon critic Ron Dellums became chairman of the House Armed Services Committee. Those who were not drawn into government tended to join the "epistemic" circles radiating out over the Hill down to Dupont Circle.

One could sense an expectation that many of the core beliefs of the peace community would soon become policy. Even those who were skeptical of Clinton, a foreign policy neophyte who vowed during the campaign to do no more than "Bush plus," had to feel some excitement. The advent of a Democratic presidency occasioned some quiet debate among progressives about how to create a responsible "left opposition" to the administration. But the prevalent feeling was that some major inroads could be made on military spending, nuclear disarmament (particularly a nuclear test ban, which Clinton endorsed in 1992), and secrecy issues, with possibly more enlightened attitudes about human rights, military intervention, and foreign development aid as well.

Like most things in the Clinton presidency, these expectations were largely dashed, although the disappointment was not complete. Small gains were made, but the coming of the Republican Congress in 1995 degraded the possibility of persisting with a progressive agenda after Clinton's first two years. For the most part, nuclear issues were handled responsibly by the new administration, aiming as they did to deal with the thorny matter of the old Soviet arsenal. The rogues festered, but Iraq was a Reagan-Bush creation and North Korea was deftly maneuvered by Ambassador Robert Gallucci, with the strong assist from Jimmy Carter. The Non-Proliferation Treaty was successfully renewed in 1995, again with a strong assist from the NGO community that had so assiduously been cultivated by the Rockefeller Brothers Fund in particular. But other initiatives foundered. Spending went down, but the choices in the military budget continued to favor large, expensive systems like the F-22 fighter jet, a foolish waste attributable to the power of the defense industry. Military secrecy and still-enormous expenditures for the CIA scarcely underwent any revision at all.

Few innovative initiatives rose in the Clinton years to advance the momentum of disarmament started in the late 1980s. In part, this was an "institutional" failure: The Clintonites showed little taste for utilizing the various levers of influence available to them, levers that could have counterbalanced a Pentagon that the president was obviously afraid to confront. A glaring example was the office of the science adviser, which during the 1960s and 1970s was a powerful post of influence under Jerome Wiesner and Frank Press. Under Clinton, it was all but invisible, with no initiatives and even an adviser whose name is difficult to recall.[7] Another was the Arms Control and Disarmament Agency, the longtime advocate of restraint that was an independent agency, reporting directly to the president, until its status was diminished (relegated to the dust bin of the State Department) in a deal with Senator Jesse Helms for which the administration received nothing tangible in return.

The shortage of vision for a post–Cold War world was manifest everywhere in the Clinton government, with very few exceptions. (This shortage alone should have toppled the stubborn belief of many funders that educating and placing people at high levels of decision making was the best possible route to policy change.) The promise of a Democratic White House and Congress, and the invitation to so many friends to serve, had the additional deleterious effect of gutting much of the critical thinking and energies that remained in the peace community at the beginning of this amazingly new, post-Soviet period. It is not an overstatement to claim that the work of this community on these many issues in the previous dozen years made it possible for a new president and Congress to disassemble the old national security state—at least to open it to new ideas and more democratic governance. That this opening was not exploited is simply and sadly a failure of national leadership, namely, a leader philosophically barren and unwilling to consider how the new world he inherited could be reshaped for human rights, disarmament, the prevention of conflict, and global economic equity.

The lacunae in Clinton's foreign policy aptitude became conspicuous when the new president addressed his first major foreign policy crisis, the terrible civil war in Yugoslavia. At that time, the war in Bosnia and Herzegovina had already claimed tens of thousands of lives, with refugees swamping the new democracies of Eastern Europe. Cyrus Vance and David Owen, operating under the auspices of the United Nations and the European Union (EU), had just completed a negotiation between the Bosnian parties—Muslims, Serbs, and Croats—that would, in effect, divide up the small country into ethnic "cantons." The Vance-Owen plan was riddled with problems, but it had the chance of stopping the killing and creating a legal framework to deal with its flaws in a climate of peace, however tense. The Clinton team backed away from the plan—spooked, perhaps, by General Colin Powell's outlandish effort to subvert the plan, publicly stating it was unworkable just before Clinton was inaugurated—and said it wanted to try to negotiate a better scheme. (The liberal foreign policy community was split on the Vance-Owen plan as well, with some declaiming it as endorsing ethnic cleansing.) Of course, nothing was negotiated, and the ineffectual secretary of state, Warren Christopher, stumbled through more than two years while the carnage escalated. UN presence in Bosnia was wholly ineffectual, often embarrassingly so. The European Union stood by with equal cowardice. NATO was nowhere to be seen. The Organization for Security and Cooperation in Europe (OSCE), the much-vaunted protector of human rights ideals across all of Europe, did not seize the initiative to halt the bloodletting. Until the genocide at Srebrenica in the summer of 1995 finally confronted these agencies with an outrage that could not be ignored—an awareness greatly amplified by NGOs like Refugees International, which used the news media to keep stories of the massacre on the front burner—the war in Bosnia, which finally claimed two hundred thousand lives and two million refugees, raged on in the absence of an international will to stop it.

This tragedy, for me, was eye-opening. So many of us had placed our philosophical faith in "collective security" as the alternative to the U.S.–USSR dementia. The end of the Cold War seemed to herald the day of multilateralism—the emergence of the United Nations, in particular, as the instrument of peacemaking and peacekeeping, possessing everything from diplomacy and aid to sanctions and military force. Indeed, much of grant making by peace donors was dedicated to cooperative security and multilateralism. But in Bosnia, four multilateral agencies—UN, NATO, EU, OSCE—had failed utterly to confront the killers and stop a war in Europe. Here were the wealthiest, most sophisticated of international organizations; for the three European institutions, no major conflict had stained their soil for nearly a half century. The idea that the major powers would fill the gap was equally naïve: The United States was failing to act under both Bush and Clinton, and Britain, France, Italy, and Germany all showed no inclination to step forward. Soon followed the debacle in Somalia, where U.S. troops went on a calamitous head-hunting mission, and the next big outrage, Rwanda, where the UN was forewarned of a genocide, but the major powers—including the United States—intentionally submerged the warnings. Close to one million people were macheted to death and the whole of central Africa was tossed into bloody turmoil.

What became clear to me was a disheartening fact: the idea of competent collective security was something bordering on delusion. Yes, one could imagine a more effective UN, an OSCE with teeth, and a NATO in the service of something more than area defense. But these qualities were not reality. If anything, the major powers were moving in the opposite direction, toward a "re-nationalization" of foreign policy, a new emphasis on satisfying national priorities rather than supranational ideals. The major powers were exhausted by the Cold War, and the will to act in concert was scant.

This fact was driven home by a meeting Search for Common Ground sponsored with Winston Foundation support in Italy in the spring of 1993. John Marks, the founder and executive director of Search, came to me the previous December to see if we could think of something to do about Bosnia. It was a typically cheeky thing for Marks to propose, but it was appealing precisely because so few good ideas were afloat. We decided to start with two small meetings of "stakeholders" to sort out what might be done. At the first, in a lovely twelfth-century church in Spoleto, Italy, leading members of the policy planning staffs of the United States, Britain, Germany, France, and Italy met with a number of intellectuals, such as our host, Mario Zucconi of the Centro Studi di Politica Internazionale. The conclusion of the policy advisers was twofold: first, our individual nations couldn't be expected to intervene militarily, because the situation was not a "vital interest" and our nations' publics wouldn't support such action; second, if NGOs wanted to do something useful, they could build institutions in Macedonia and Kosovo to prevent "spillover"—the spread of the ethnic strife to these multiethnic provinces of the former Yugoslavia. (A second meeting, in Virginia, brought activists from those lands, and one result was Search's excellent mission in Macedonia.)

If the major powers were willfully disengaged, and the multilateral agencies were controlled by the major powers, the prospects for decisive, timely, inventive action to prevent conflict appeared quite bleak. Yet here we were facing the primary source of war and disruption in the world. With the bilateral rivalry dead, the chances for a catastrophic nuclear war were near zero (apart from the still-worrisome chance of an accident). Here, instead, was the crucible of conflict: The wars, often fought with remarkably low-tech weapons, were spurred by ethnic, tribal, and religious divisions, sentiments cruelly manipulated by corrupt or even criminal regimes. These "small" conflicts, moreover, had the potential to incite disaster. Chechnya, Bosnia, and, later, Kosovo riled Moscow and set it against the West; Kashmir threatened to erupt into war between India and Pakistan; the Kurds' strivings for independence confronted U.S. ally Turkey and U.S. adversary Iraq and upset a cogent policy in the region; the Chiapas rebellion sparked a crisis of legitimacy in America's enormous neighbor, and so on. These were not just sad little affairs to pull at the heart strings of the world's do-gooders. These wars were troubling both in the magnitude of their violence and the breadth of their consequences. It was, quite apparently, the way the world was going, the future of war and peace.

8

THE CIVIL SOCIETY REVOLUTION

At the time the Winston Foundation was reassessing its program following the Cold War, a phenomenon of extraordinary breadth and power was surfacing—the growth and central significance of civil society. The revolutions in Eastern Europe in 1989 were largely a triumph of civil society—that "space" between the state and the family in which free political association, ideas, and organizations are hatched and operate. At the 1992 UN conference on sustainability in Rio de Janeiro, the pivotal influence of environmental organizations was evident as well, signaling a new, global dimension to civil society. The population groups I encountered through the Kendall Foundation demonstrated the variety and rootedness of this phenomenon, ranging from small nonprofit or village-based organizations to enterprises with worldwide reach, some dedicated to women's empowerment and others to sophisticated research in multilateral agencies, some writing scripts for soap operas in Mexico or India, and others organizing caravans of African men and women to stage proselytizing puppet shows and to distribute condoms across the continent. To suddenly see this phenomenon (which had been building for years, of course) for what it was and could be—a new force for the prevention of conflict—was like having the proverbial scales fall from my eyes.

The organizations of civil society in Africa, the Balkans, and other places where we soon became involved were the counterparts of the nonprofits we were funding in the United States. It is one of the peculiarities of American political culture, a culture that does not fully grasp the significance of its own civil society, apart from a superficial nod to "voluntarism." In political science and journalism, successful advocacy NGOs like the Sierra Club or the Vietnam Veterans Foundation are labeled "interest groups" and are lumped together with the Petroleum Institute or the American Medical Association as just another lobbying group seeking to advance its own narrow interests. What we were seeing in the zones of conflict, however, was something different from "interest groups" or single-issue advocates. It was a much more inclusive and operational form of organization than was typically found in the United States, at least in the peace community. One could see the immense energy and inventiveness of these groups in places thought to be moribund or backwards in any number of endeavors—disarmament, human rights, women's issues, humanitarian aid and development, democracy-building, and scores of other causes. Yet it was little recognized as such a transformative force.

"The twentieth century has been a time of immense social innovation," write Lester Salamon and Helmut Anheier, leading scholars of civil society who teach at Johns Hopkins University. "Paradoxically, however, one of the social innovations for which the twentieth century may deserve to be best known is still largely hidden from view, obscured by a set of concepts that cloud its existence . . . That innovation is the civil society sector, the plethora of private, nonprofit and nongovernmental organizations that have emerged in recent decades in virtually every corner of the world to provide vehicles through which citizens can exercise individual initiative in the private pursuit of public purposes."[1] As Salamon and Anheier point out, the number of NGOs that perform vital services in industrialized societies is breathtaking—large percentages of houses constructed, day care provided, hospitals kept open, education given, and so on, spring from NGO sources. The head of an umbrella group for European nonprofits claimed to me that between the Atlantic and the Urals, six million NGOs were operating. And these statistics reflect activity only in Europe. In the Third World, NGOs may be fewer in number, but governments are often weak and poor, or nearly dysfunctional, and civil society organizations can play an even larger role, replacing, in effect, the government itself in many key sectors.

While the service-provider aspect of civil society was impressive, the dimension of greater interest to me was the innovative way NGOs were approaching difficult and controversial problems, conflict in particular. They seemed to offer a fresh, new approach to what was indisputably a new set of problems for global security. The contours of the Cold War were bilateral, technical, and economic: concerns and activity flowed along those lines. But the conflicts that were arising or reemerging in the 1990s were none of those things. They tended to be internal. The types of technologies used seemed almost incidental. And the financial costs of the wars, while unfortunate, were far less troubling than the extravagant human costs. Moreover, these conflicts tended to draw in the major powers and thereby became significant and often disruptive items on the international security agenda. Yet, as noted, the big powers and the multilateral agencies were not coping well with the wars in Bosnia, Eastern Slavonia, Somalia, Rwanda, Tajikistan, and so on. The possibility of a "third force" that might alter the dynamics of these wretched wars was immensely attractive.

In thinking through a funding program that would utilize this outburst of global, public interest activity, I had to search through a set of rationales that would answer skepticism about a sharp departure from what we had been doing for several years. Why move away from grassroots activism in the United States? Why such confidence in the phenomenon of civil society? And, even if those kinds of doubts could be relieved, how could a small foundation, spending no more than two million dollars annually, hope to reshape these venues of conflict?

A SMALL DIGRESSION ON THEORY

While I cannot claim to have worked out a cogent theoretical answer to those sorts of questions in the early 1990s, my philosophical instincts were alert to the reasons why we should shift our funding attention so dramatically. This reasoning came to affect our nuclear disarmament program in the mid-1990s as well.

Drawing my attention at first were the possibilities in track two diplomacy. Governments often failed to convene the relevant parties to a conflict—it was politically too risky to be seen with insurgents in many of the most intractable wars, or the conditions for dialogue were too narrow and rigid. NGOs had no such limitations, and this fundamental truth had been demonstrated time and again during the Cold War. A freelance negotiator like Robert White, the former ambassador to El Salvador who heads the Center for International Policy, could access rebels not only because he had no political shackles but because he was a trusted interlocutor. And, indeed, White (among many others) played a significant role in brokering meetings that helped formulate the peace accords signed in El Salvador in 1992. But track two is an instrument, not a strategy of change. Even conflict resolution must be regarded in a broader context of how positive change happens.

What the concept of civil society provided was this context. In fact, of course, we had been operating in American civil society all along. In this civil society, which is as old as the republic, individuals freely associating into groups—unions, clubs, professional associations, single-issue organizations, et cetera—act to influence social institutions, public attitudes, and the political system. Their action repertoires may vary widely, from publishing to lobbying to protesting to disobeying and many things in between, but they form their ideas and action agendas in the free space of society. Certain powerful players and ideas may come to dominate civil society, such as the ideology of "free enterprise" in the United States, and may act in concert with state institutions to enforce a kind of consensus or uniformity of belief. But civil society can rarely be dominated for long; it will almost always give rise to dissident ideas and demands, as long as civil society itself is allowed to exist. Authoritarian regimes tend to suppress civil society for precisely that reason, which was particularly true of Soviet communism.

To quote a somewhat more academic definition: *Civil society* is "a sphere of social interaction between economy and state, composed above all of the intimate sphere (the family), the sphere of associations (especially voluntary associations), social movements, and forms of public communication. Modern civil society is created through forms of self-constitution and self-mobilization. It is institutionalized and generalized through laws, and especially subjective rights, that stabilize social differentiation." It is different from the "political society" of parties and elections and legislatures, and separate from the economic activity and institutions, though all three interact.[2] Many leading political philosophers—Friedrich Hegel, Karl Marx, Antonio Gramsci, Hannah Arendt, and Jürgen Habermas, among others—wrote extensively about the relationship between the state, the individual, and civil society. For the most part, civil society has been seen as the grounds upon which contending ideas and interests vie for attention and influence. It is also the culture in which new ideas and social movements are incubated, hatched, and mature. It is seen variously as a place where hegemonic power (the state, the business, or the corporation) can co-opt dissent and grievances, or, by contrast, the only platform to counter such hegemonic power.

One could see the nuclear freeze campaign as a classic social movement arising in civil society—in church basements, school rooms, and alternative newspapers—that directly challenged the hegemonic ideology of nuclear deterrence and the hegemonic power of the military-industrial complex. (One of the criticisms of the freeze is that it prematurely entered "political society" and lost its power as a social, cultural, and moral force.) All of our grantees were of civil society, whether they were grassroots activists, think tanks, periodicals, or professional groups. Each was operating in that public sphere of free activity, aiming to shape attitudes and change issues of war and peace.

Leftists in the United States and Europe harbored a rather ambivalent attitude about civil society, however, in part because for so many decades the state was viewed as the ultimate prize in effecting social change. In this view, it is the state (or government) that has the power to make right what is wrong, and only the state; the object of social and political movements, therefore, is to capture the instruments and institutions of state power. Indeed, to some degree a classic confrontation emerged in which some liberals would argue that society itself (family, church, school, free press, et cetera) had to be protected from the state, and should have an autonomous existence, while leftists saw all such institutions as either retrograde or subject to the need for revolutionary alteration. This statist view was on the wane even before the Soviet Union collapsed; few self-respecting leftists after 1953 would look to the USSR as any sort of model, of course, but the theoretical lines were nonetheless drawn. Marxists were obviously outmoded with respect to their views on this point, but they continued to exert a strong influence that permeates much debate to this day.

What occurred in the late 1980s, particularly in the captive nations of Eastern Europe, returned attention to the transformative dynamics inherent in civil society, particularly because the transformations were taking place in a system where civil society was not meant to exist. The most remarkable of these developments, the trade union Solidarity in Poland, not only formed in opposition to the comprehensive state, with a set of "self-limiting" or negotiable political claims, but it also sought at the same time to nurture civil society itself. Other instances of this phenomenon were also visible at the time, not only in Czechoslovakia and Hungary, but also notably in South Africa. These revolutions succeeded because of enlightened leadership (Gorbachev, Nelson Mandela, and so on) and democratic struggle "from below," and because global civil society was already at work. One of the pivotal concepts of civil society is the right to *have* a civil society, to have freedom of association and speech and so on, independent of political or economic systems, and such a rights-based perspective had for forty years been evolving as a pillar of international norms. This human rights revolution was energized not by the major powers, which largely resisted or ignored it, but by a few NGOs that insisted upon new standards of conduct that gradually took hold. White South Africa and Communist Poland had to "behave" when confronted by its civil society opposition because the world would no longer tolerate these states—as it had before—brutally suppressing widely accepted ideals of fairness and participation. Civil society, both global and national, had nurtured new institutions, leadership, ideas, actions, values, and expectations. They made governments of all kinds accountable. And what could have been the bloodiest of confrontations was resolved not only peacefully, but justly. This accomplishment was rather impressive.

Virtually ignored in discussions of civil society today is, in my view, the very embodiment of much that is envisioned for civil society—

Mohandas K. Gandhi. One could simply list his unique achievements as conclusive evidence of his primacy: a founder of the antiapartheid movement in South Africa, the leader of the social movement in India for independence from Britain, the founder of the political party that democratically ruled India following independence for four decades, and an originator of nonviolent social action as a primary instrument of social and political change, which inspired a diverse lot that includes Nelson Mandela, Martin Luther King Jr. and Malcolm X, Lech Walesa and Vaçlav Havel, Mubarak Awad, and innumerable others. Among Gandhi's more significant philosophical contributions to what we now call civil society (a term he didn't use) is the relationship between the demands for rights and identity, and the obligations of action and citizenship. During the anti-imperialist struggle in India, he frequently distinguished between independence and a pivotal concept of *swaraj*, an Indian term that was central to his life and action: "The root meaning of *swaraj* is self-rule. *Swaraj* may, therefore, be rendered as disciplined rule from within . . . 'Independence' has no such limitation. Independence may mean license to do as you like. *Swaraj* is positive. Independence is negative . . . The word *swaraj* is a sacred word, a Vedic word, meaning self-rule and self-restraint, and not freedom from all restraint which 'independence' often means." One could usefully speculate on the acute relevance of such a simple notion in today's libertine environment, but it was a particularly powerful principle in colonial India. In this peculiar word he incorporated what today would be called *empowerment*, an utterly revolutionary idea in his time and place, as well as inclusiveness with regard to class, color, sex, and religion—equally revolutionary concepts. Of course, he did not just theorize, he acted. And by combining this vigorous citizenship with his *satyagraha*—nonviolent action—he achieved that remarkable thing, the self-inducing, self-expanding sphere of political and social freedom and work, with the acts of resistance bolstering the sense of power and democratic entitlement of the participants. And this on behalf of a range of demands that one would still see as visionary: equality between sexes and classes; free education; a living wage for all workers; protection of the culture, language, and "scripts" of all minorities; reductions in military expenditures; appropriately scaled technology for indigenous manufacture; state control of vital industry, and so on.[3] This set of demands was not tepid, nor was it a mere outrage at the base rudeness of English overlords. It was the intentional creation of a self-regulating sphere of social and political activity, with an emphasis on autonomy, dignity, democracy, and universality.

This short round of philosophy underscores four essential points. The first is to draw a distinction between action in civil society that is aimed at gaining something from the state, typically some legislation, and action to enlarge and vitalize civil society itself as a counterterrain to the state. The narrower project of politics, lobbying, polling, image-crafting, et cetera, is often sterile and isolated, disconnected from the real lives and concerns of people. It also means that there is no formal difference between, say, an arms-control lobbying group and the National Rifle Association, or a scholar who proposes "X" and another scholar who proposes "anti-X." Second, all theorists see social movements as the *sine qua non* of a conscientious civil society. Social movements provide authenticity, energy, reexamination of values, challenges to state power, and the like, that not only make civil society vibrant, creative, and communitarian, but also provide it with a fluid means to fend off domination by the powerful. And, of course, social movements present demands for change, for political "goods." Third, civil society is separate from the economy, and provides a platform for activists to confront economic institutions just as they might challenge institutions of the state—with a reforming, normative zeal. Gandhi's emphasis on autonomy and self-reliance (recall his celebrated habit of spinning cotton thread) was very much an integral part of his concept and practice of social action, and economic relations were to be as fair, inclusive, and purposeful as social relations. His famous salt satyagraha was first and foremost a protest against British imperialism (their tax on salt), but he chose among many British abuses an *economic* relationship to mobilize the nation. Finally, because relations in civil society are meant to be democratic, inclusive, discursive, and the like, conflicts are to be resolved peaceably; the exercise of arbitrary power, certainly the use of violence, is anathema to civil society, and in this implicit embrace of conflict resolution is a method for political relations within and outside the nation-state.

It should not be surprising, then, that it is in civil society and among the activist NGOs that the universal principles of democracy, openness, equality, and peace are most likely to be protected, as are the polity's obligations to the future. National governments are, by their nature, dedicated to protecting *state* interests or national goals, which explains why, among other reasons, traditional diplomacy does not consistently strive for universal values. The pursuit of national interests can and does involve (and, some would say, necessitate) a resort to violence, inequity, secrecy, and the like. The business corporation is dedicated to economic goals, profit and expansion, and nothing else. Religions also act in particularistic ways. In civil society is the greatest potential to consistently uphold progressive values. Where civil society is weak, lacking vibrancy, or dominated by nationalistic ideology, it does not fulfill this potential. Among the achievements of global movements like human rights and women's empowerment, however, is the infusion of their values into the civil societies of nearly every country in the world, and it is this phenomenon, and this tremendous potential, that excites the imagination and stirs a concrete hope for positive, transformative action for peace and justice.

CAPTURING THE CIVIL SOCIETY MOMENT

Translating this hope into a funding program was easier said than done. The Winston Foundation was small. There were others beginning to show interest in these potentialities, and indeed some private and public donors had for years been supporting, whether consciously or not, the development of civil society. The Ford Foundation and others among the big, international funders had long invested in economic development, scholarly enterprise, and a smattering of other such pieces of the civil society fabric abroad. These investments for the most part were grants to "modernize" the countries, cultivating utilitarian expertise or applying useful methods of water and soil conservation, farming techniques (*e.g.*, the "green revolution"), birth control, legal education, and the like. They could have the effect of strengthening the state, with the intention of nurturing good governance, and creating epistemic communities in the intelligentsia. But despite some patronizing and ham-handed practices, the net effect enhanced the evolution of independent civil society via education, community projects, and transnational networks.

The difference at the end of the 1980s was the advent of civil society in so many countries—formerly communist and "underdeveloped" nations alike—as *independent* terrains of social and political action. Again, this development had been happening for many years, but the coincidence of the end of Soviet communism and the advancement of the communications revolution, together with the rapid emergence of transnational networks of environmentalists, human rights advocates, and others, brought this phenomenon to a new height of viability and visibility. It was novel in its depth, its ubiquity, and its connectedness.

As I understood it then, we should seek ways to support the organizations involved in utilizing the assets of civil society in areas of conflict to promote the infrastructure of what I liked to call the NGO revolution. I also intended to support "experiments" in NGO peace building—in effect, to expand and verify the utility of the action repertoires of these organizations. In fact, one of the encouraging prospects offered by these civil society actors was that they had many tools at their disposal. One could see, in virtually every venue of incipient or actual conflict, NGOs dedicated variously to the early warning of conflict, advocacy (human rights, refugee relief, women's empowerment, and disarmament), dialogue between adversaries, economic development, independent news media, mobilization of the afflicted, and appeals to the more powerful in the world, among other instruments. The presence of a rich and varied civil society seemed to exert a moderating effect on the state as well, for their eyes and ears provided a check on power and lying and corruption that no official institution could. What I found particularly inventive was the way many such groups moved beyond pleading to governments to "do something," to doing something themselves. The many manifestations of dialogue certainly fit into this self-help mold, as did the creation of independent news media, particularly radio, news services, actual periodicals, and Internet sites. It was a profoundly hopeful sign in an otherwise dispiriting age of spineless leaders tolerating mindless slaughter.

I returned to the Winston board with the requisite options for a funding program for our final seven years. While I presented without prejudice the two options—the military economy and cooperative security—I was pleased that the board saw the latter category as the more alluring. The military economy increasingly struck me as being similar to the arms-control project itself—a rather narrow technical definition of activity that addressed a side effect instead of more fundamental causes of injustice in the world. Within the category of cooperative security, I could construct a program that used the NGO revolution and confronted the roots of conflict. With particular support from trustees like Melinda Scrivner, who early on expressed a preference for conflict resolution, and Bob Allen, who frequently voiced his concern about more basic questions of human behavior and mass violence, I felt confident we could take the Winston Foundation in a new direction that did not violate the spirit of the enterprise conceived by Bob Scrivner.

By early 1993, a few months after moving the Winston operations from Boston to Washington, I presented to the trustees for their approval the final memorandum on guidelines, the culmination of eighteen months of reassessment. I emphasized the continuing need for disarmament activity, and expressed doubts about the efficacy and courage of the multilateral agencies. In beginning the case for concentrating on what we came to call conflict prevention, I reminded them that we had supported a number of projects right from the beginning that were quite similar to the more ambitious agenda I was proposing. We supported several "unofficial diplomacy" initiatives, for example, including the Natural Resources Defense Council (NRDC) verification project. This sort of work was now being called "track two diplomacy," a phrase coined by Joseph Montville, a leading theorist and practitioner, that conveyed its difference from official track one negotiations.

But track two was about policy, or preventing conflict, or some other substantive matter, distinguishing it from "citizen diplomacy," that could be simple, nonsubstantive exchanges between the peoples of countries in conflict—a common practice during the Cold War.

In my memo to the trustees, I set this funding agenda in the context of civil society. "We also recognized," I wrote, "at a fairly early stage, the significance of 'civil society' in the transformation of Eastern Europe and elsewhere. It is in civil society—the sociopolitical culture independent of the state (or party)—where NGOs operate, and the successful revolutions in Poland, Czechoslovakia, and Hungary occurred precisely because a rudimentary, underground civil society flourished under communism and provided the political culture, ideas, and leaders to stimulate and carry out the changes. Grantees such as Rob Manoff, Joanne Landy, and the Helsinki Citizens Assembly were visionary proponents of building civil society as a path to peace." We were linking, in this new program, the new dynamism of civil society, and methods like track two diplomacy, with a substantive goal—the prevention, transformation, or resolution of conflict. "It is predicated on the belief that private actors—mainly activist NGOs—can play a significant part in averting war, stopping incipient conflict, and reconciling warring parties after war ends. Importantly, we also assert these abilities can become a permanent, pervasive feature of global political life." I then listed the specific repertoires I had in mind:

- deploying track two delegations to the endangered areas, where direct mediation can be pursued;
- using skilled and experienced practitioners who train people in the afflicted region in the techniques of conflict prevention;
- integrating these techniques into the programs of a wide variety of NGOs, and providing data and opportunities through NGO networks;
- building institutions around the world that are dedicated to teaching, training, and practicing conflict prevention;
- enhancing the receptivity to conflict prevention through the reconstruction of civil society in selected regions;
- working with governments and multilateral organizations to encourage official policies of conflict prevention and support for unofficial efforts; and
- using broad public education, mainly through the news media, to acquaint the engaged public of the value of conflict prevention.

"The durable legacy we can leave," I concluded, "is the proliferation of conflict prevention skills, institutions, acceptability, and practice. Because so few foundations are involved, because the field itself is relatively young, and because the conflicts we face seem so impervious to balance-of-power geopolitics, the opportunity to have a creative, lasting impact is palpable. A funding program would support the best players we can find . . . , building indigenous capacity for conflict prevention throughout the world. Such capacity is indispensable to our goal of perpetuality." This strategy, I argued, was one of "investing broadly in a *capacity for peacebuilding*, . . . the wisest course toward the 21st century, because we simply cannot anticipate the precise nature of issues of war and peace."

The trustees embraced this program enthusiastically, which was a little surprising. They were for the most part a group honed on U.S. activism and advocacy. Leslie Dunbar, as a former director of the Field Foundation, was particularly oriented to American-based movement politics. John Adams, who headed NRDC, and Alice Tepper Marlin, who directed the Council on Economic Priorities, were deeply involved in disarmament advocacy, which was being downgraded (though not abandoned) as a foundation priority. Roy Carlin, a New York attorney, expressed skepticism from time to time about the advisability or even legality of unofficial diplomacy. Al Sims was clearly more interested in the possibilities of official multilateral action. But all of them set aside their misgivings to seize what they apparently saw as a fresh new direction, possibly encompassing the boldness they had long desired even if its precise shape was unexpected.

These ideas paralleled a fresh emphasis in liberal foreign policy circles on "preventive action," a phrase that was even adopted for a time, without discernable impact, by Secretary of State Warren Christopher. The Council on Foreign Relations, the Carnegie Corporation, the Center for Strategic and International Studies, and a few other such institutions embraced prevention in foreign affairs. For the most part, this policy meant no more than acting earlier, being more anticipatory, and savoring the chance to prevent a war rather than having to clean up afterwards. The paradigm shift did not sink in very deeply, even as the examples of the need for prevention proliferated in Burundi, Zaire, Kosovo, East Timor, and other sad places. I recall an especially representative moment during a conference at the State Department sponsored by Carnegie via its newly minted Commission on Preventing Deadly Conflict. One of the speakers was Richard Haass, a Bush-era official who was soon to become the head of the Brookings foreign policy program. Haass said that preventive diplomacy was nothing new, since diplomats always tried to prevent conflict. This statement was disingenuous. Diplomats act first and foremost in the interests of the state—which is what they're paid to do—and if that means going to war, then so be it. Traditional diplomacy has little to do with universal values.

Washington's brief infatuation with preventive diplomacy was no more than a plea to be more effective. As long as it was tied to government institutions, the concept would be limited by the ever-powerful need to satisfy "national interests," that is economic and security prerogatives, through the use of the state's instruments—the military, economic coercion, and the like.

Such a framework for prevention was not what many of us on the outside were interested in. The civil society revolution offered to us a more durable, reliable, and moral instrument of expressing and implementing universal values of peace and justice. Now we had to go find, or forge, the tools of that vision.

9

BUILDING THE HOUSE OF PEACE

A revealing anecdote is told by the Israeli journalist, Amos Oz, in his story about how the Oslo peace accords came about. The 1993 agreement, which set the course for a comprehensive peace between Israel and the Palestinians, was in part the result of a track two initiative by Yair Hirschfield and Ron Pundik, two Jerusalem-based freelance diplomats. Hirschfield and Pundik were able to establish contacts with the Palestine Liberation Organization at a time when Israeli officials, even those in the Labour government in the early 1990s, dared not do. These contacts led to a series of unofficial negotiations, secret talks hosted and facilitated by a quasi-private Norwegian institute. The result, months later, was the remarkable breakthrough for peace in this most vexing conflict. The Norwegians told the State Department of the progress of the talks, including the draft treaty, but the Americans "did not believe we could pull it off," as one of the Norwegians told Oz. "So we stopped telling them. We felt, Why should we bother? And they didn't ask any questions." The Norwegian foreign minister finally briefed Warren Christopher, the U.S. secretary of state, on the agreement. "Christopher is said to have had trouble getting his mind around the idea that Norway might succeed where Washington could not," Oz reports. And, one hastens to add, he would be even more befuddled by the central role of the "amateur peacemakers" in Oslo.[1]

The Oslo process triumphed not only because of Pundik and Hirschfeld. Hundreds, if not thousands, of people in many countries helped to pave the way for the peace. People like Herbert Kelman, a Harvard professor of psychology, who ran problem-solving workshops between Israelis and Palestinians for twenty-five years. Or the American Friends Service Committee (AFSC), which built relationships in the region for decades. Or Search for Common Ground's Middle East Initiative, which brought elites from around the region to meet regularly and nurture both trust and ideas for solutions, some of which, like Kelman's and AFSC's, were deftly infused into the official negotiating process. Peace Now, the Israeli NGO, and other advocacy groups helped to argue the "land for peace" equation and build the public demand for an agreement that made all the track two diplomacy fertile.

Not all of the conflict resolution work undertaken by NGOs has such a remarkable outcome. But if one scratches the surface of any conflict, if one looks into the grinding gears of a peace process, civil society groups are visible. In Mozambique, it was the Communitá di Sant'Egidio, a Catholic humanitarian organization, that facilitated the talks in Rome that ended the brutal civil war. In Northern Ireland, countless NGOs built the relationships and created the solutions to move toward the accords. In South Africa, nonviolent social movements and hundreds of community groups created pressure for an end to apartheid, and built bonds among parties, tribes, and liberal whites to work together. Other, less spectacular gains were made in the Caucasus, in the former Yugoslavia, in Central America, and even the still-violent Burundi, Sierra Leone, Angola, Tajikistan, Colombia, Mexico, Turkey, Cambodia, Sri Lanka, and other places. In these venues, civil society actors have taken a leading role by using the tools of prevention: early warning of conflict from aid workers, NGOs, and others "on the ground"; convening dialogues between antagonists; creating new media to educate the population in areas at risk of conflict; monitoring the tense areas for human rights violations and other signs of trouble; alerting the global news media to incipient conflicts, which may force political leaders to act; utilizing the good offices of clergy, most obviously where religion is an ostensible cause of strife; and so on. The sheer numbers and variety of NGOs that can and do perform "conflict-resolution" tasks are enormous; thousands of such groups throughout the world, some with global reach, but many small and local. The engaged groups aren't always formed to deal with conflict; instead, they may be dedicated to women's empowerment, environmental protection, economic justice, educational reform, or any number of other concerns. But they come to see conflict as a social destroyer that needs their skills and attention. The variety and density of this global and national civil society—while potentially confusing—ensures numerous points of contact for antagonists, ample early warning and human rights monitoring, and, not least, a strong moral voice for doing the right thing.

In the scheme of international relations, the rationale for this NGO involvement is straightforward. Governments very often are politically constrained from dealing directly with adversaries. Or the government has been corrupted. The adversary likewise has constraints, perhaps a rigid commitment to a militant ideology or a leadership prone to violence and vulnerable to prosecution. International mediators (who tend to avoid involvement in civil wars) may be helpful in these circumstances, of course, but it's the rare case when a UN special envoy or some Scandinavian foreign minister can simply walk into a violent civil war and start negotiations. A set of conditions must be created for the high-profile mediators to have any chance of success. In rare cases, the major powers may coerce the warriors to bargain, as was the case with the Dayton accords that ended the Bosnian war in 1995; but the expenditure of the capital—political, military, and economic—necessary to force such compliance is typically unaffordable. More often, we are seeing conflicts being addressed by civil society groups that have few if any political constraints, that do not have suspicious interests in the outcome, and that forward values that supersede narrow and often reactionary ideologies. They represent, symbolically and at times literally, the victims of the conflict. Such organizations have a comparative advantage as peacemakers: they are indigenous, they are unencumbered, they can behave fairly, and they seek a just peace that conforms to universal norms.

"I believe that the nature and characteristics of contemporary conflict suggest the need for a set of concepts and approaches that go beyond traditional statist diplomacy," writes John Paul Lederach, one of the world's leading theorist-practitioners. "Building peace in today's conflicts calls for long-term commitment to establishing an infrastructure across the levels of a society, an infrastructure that empowers the resources for reconciliation from within that society and maximizes the contribution from the outside. In short, constructing the house of peace relies on a foundation of multiple actors and activities aimed at achieving and sustaining reconciliation."[2]

It was this set of concepts that framed the Winston Foundation's philanthropy in conflict prevention. A very few private foundations pursued a similar course. We encountered with the new direction of our program a new set of philanthropic partners, NGOs, experts, obstacles, and opportunities.

THE TWIN TRACKS OF PREVENTING CONFLICT

We plunged into the field during that early evening meeting I had with John Marks of Search for Common Ground in late 1992, when we brainstormed about the unfolding horror in Bosnia and Herzegovina. That project was in many ways typical of how Winston approached the enormous and varied challenges of conflict in the 1990s: We invested in a good "athlete" who could create a versatile, adaptable structure for defining an addressable problem and employing action repertoires to get at it. John Marks did just that: The meetings of elites in Spoleto and Virginia defined a clear problem—spillover from the Bosnia nightmare—that was amenable to civil society actors. The concrete result, which we also funded in its formative years (as did the Carnegie Corporation), was a Search for Common Ground mission in Macedonia, a former Yugoslavian province that had a mixed, and tense, ethnic composition. Kosovo, it was thought, was too difficult to address in the same way because Slobodan Milosevic would not tolerate a mission in Pristina, a decision I later regretted. But the Skopje venture flowered and prospered. Its work included back channel facilitation during the imbroglio with Greece (which objected to the use of the name and some symbols of Macedonia), series of meetings between politicians, education projects for children, multiethnic news reporting training with journalists, and other activities. The Skopje project was not the only NGO activity in the country, of course, but it was quite early and prominent. It connected elite-level discourse with popularizing activities. And it enhanced the work of other NGOs and the international agencies in Macedonia.

The design of that project went far to answer doubts I long harbored about conflict resolution. Two aspects of the method bothered me. The first one focused on the widely held image of conflict resolution as a foolishly idealistic waste of time. It seemed to be too soft for a hard world. My fears on this image surfaced regularly, not least when we funded a television program on conflict prevention that turned out to be a fuzzy-focus series of images of children holding hands and singing something like "It's a Small World After All." (The producer of that show did not get another grant.) An unfortunate number of conflict-resolution projects tend toward this feel-good sensibility, something like one in four. There's a place for such activity, but it was not at the Winston Foundation table. Conflict prevention techniques, I knew, could and should be "muscular": dealing with the central knots of a conflict, engaging major players, coordinating with multilateral organizations, building political and social networks, and similarly concrete contributions.

The second doubt about the conflict-resolution method is a tougher one to answer: What if the parties to a conflict don't want to resolve it? I recall having debates with the method's advocates during the Cold War, among them Roger Fisher, the Harvard law professor, and Bruce Berlin, a New Mexico attorney running a U.S.–USSR project. If the antagonists reject a negotiated settlement, or even the premises of meeting, the methods of conflict resolution would seem to be irrelevant. Very few conflicts are so rigid, but the question is worth asking in every case, over and over again.

The thorny matter of whether a would-be diplomat was wanted came up early and often in our funding program, because among the first few exciting proposals we received were attempts at track two diplomacy. We supported such efforts in Burundi, Algeria, Turkey, the former Yugoslavia, the former Soviet states in the Caucasus, Mexico, and elsewhere. The endeavors in each case varied widely, however, and it is imprecise to cluster them all as track two, though they share that quality of being both unofficial in origin but with the possibility of creating opportunities to end a conflict. I came to see over time that track two, with all its inherent advantages, is nonetheless limited if not rooted deeply in the political and social conditions attending the conflict.

We spent, for example, an ample amount of money (and the time of our deputy director, Tara Magner) on a track two effort to address the uprising in Chiapas. The principal player was a very capable and experienced Latino who built relationships among the rebels and community leaders in Chiapas, and intellectuals and officials in Mexico City. He believes, and I have no reason to doubt him, that some of his work deterred an outbreak of new guerrilla violence. But ultimately his more ambitious vision—a high-level process that would both advance democratic principles and create a space for dialogue—was never realized. The failure was due in part to the lack of a viable mechanism, a structure organically and broadly drawn from Mexico's political culture, to sustain the considerable momentum he built. (It also failed because at a crucial moment the U.S. ambassador refused to release foreign aid money intended to move the project forward.) Our grantee, a man of great integrity who was invited in by the guerrillas, was a freelancer, with no institutional base, and an outsider, with no roots in Mexico—both of which were enormous liabilities against him and his mission.

The notoriety of "parachutists" became a core concern of those in the field of conflict prevention. Too many NGOs were streaming into places like Bosnia or the former USSR or the Middle East with ample amounts of good will, but no operational connections to the place. The value they offered often amounted to little more than conflict-resolution training of various kinds. Training is not enough if the methods are not connected to both the political reality of the area in conflict and the roots of the conflict. Too much relies on lawyerly mediation techniques, the "win-win" ideas that are fine in some situations, but rarely address the deeply traumatized fears and myths and grievances of people at war. The parachutists cannot be expected to have a feel for the local politics and will rarely have substantive knowledge of the historical dimensions of the conflict. Just as important, they won't stay in for the long haul, which is always required in successful conflict-resolution work. This kind of practice is more susceptible to false claims of success as well; there are a lot of Potemkin villages among these types, NGOs who assert achievements they don't deserve and rely on their very transience and remoteness to mask the empty boast.

This very sticky problem of impermanence led me to emphasize indigenous peacemaking. The civil society actors who live in zones of conflict have a much greater stake in the outcome, a simple incentive to stay and make certain their work succeeds. They know the local culture. They know the history. They must live with the consequences of their actions. The advantages are obvious. The drawbacks have equal clarity: Local peace activists may not have the resources, the wherewithal, or the political autonomy needed to be bold and creative. So investments in the infrastructure of peacemaking had to be done with an eye to these pluses and minuses.

The optimal blend seemed to be the creation of "platforms" for peacebuilding that could mobilize local human resources and link to other such platforms and NGO networks, international NGOs, officials, news media, universities, and so on. Platforms of this kind could be flexible as to mission, opportunistically embracing techniques, partnerships, and issues. Some might stress education and reconciliation, as did a promising experiment in postconflict discourse in El Salvador, called Centro Demos.[3] Others built networks of organizations and people who were committed to a peace-with-justice philosophy, and could provide skills and knowledge on an as-needed basis. This method was used to design two Winston-funded networks in Africa, one a ground-up group called the West Africa Network for Peacebuilding, the other a project of the Association of Christian Lay Centers in Africa. A Turkish-Kurdish consortium in Ankara, acronymed TOSAV, aimed to promote dialogue and problem solving through face-to-face meetings, "Democracy Radio," publications, and other outreach activities. A center in Croatia promoted interreligious dialogue, but also had training sessions, publications, and other activities. The clever activists who created these small but adroit organizations could fit the assets at their disposal to the needs of the country's troubles, and if the assets were inadequate, they could call on others in their global networks.

Among the vital contributions of civil society is the production of knowledge—among other things, information and analysis about conflict, social dislocations, economic conditions, militarization, political trends, and the like. While useful knowledge is typically generated or refined by social scientists, NGOs often furnish the raw data and insights of observation that are indispensable elements of the knowledge base. (I encouraged all our grantees to document their activities and observations precisely for this reason.) NGO activists continuously replenish the pool of empirical data, and some of them work closely with the intellectuals to maximize their mutual contributions, a replication of sorts of the relationship between critical communities and social movements described by Thomas Rochon. Platforms are beautifully compatible with this function, particularly if they are built with such a task in mind. Local NGOs and global networks do not always regard social science as a partner in these endeavors, but they miss a notable opportunity through such an omission.

Most of these platforms were constructed with the help of people from global NGO networks or research institutes. For instance, a number of small outfits in the southern Caucasus—Azerbaijan, Armenia, and Georgia—working on conflict, the environment, and other civil society concerns, were guided by a program at the University of Maryland, still others by the Initiative for Social Action & Renewal, a Washington-based organization that opened offices in the region. In some other cases, a platform has evolved from an international creation to an indigenously operated entity, such as the National Press Institute in Moscow, founded by the Center for War, Peace, and the News Media at New York University (NYU), but completely "Russified" by 1998. Still another species of the platform is the largely foreign-origin project that operates in close cooperation with local partners. In Burundi, several international NGOs, including Search for Common Ground and International Alert, work together in a loose consortium, with a strong emphasis on building the capacity of local partners, parliamentarians, and others who can move the peace process forward.

The key to a muscular profile is understanding what NGOs can and cannot accomplish. For example, because they're "on the ground" and significantly indigenous, NGOs have a comparative advantage in providing early warning of conflict, analysis of local conditions, and the like. What they cannot do is coerce, challenge military power, or sometimes even take any sides in a conflict because to do so would imperil their lives. But there is so much that NGOs can do—a thousand things more than I can mention in this brief review—that pointing to their lack of power relative to a government with an army and a treasury is a useless, diversionary quibble. What is important is deciphering appropriate roles to fit resources and circumstances, a process that is often a quandary.

Consider the group that receives word of refugee flows—very often a conflict's canary-in-the-coal-mine—and investigates further to find sizable human rights violations by a central government in a region of the country that is ethnically different from the ruling clique in the capital. One of the group's major assets may be a connection to the international news media, which could provide a warning of an impending genocide that then alerts the world and, possibly, some action by the international community. But such an alert could be viewed by the country's rulers as a lethal challenge to their authority. Moreover, should the group hope to resolve the conflict through mediation or dialogue, its neutrality would be poisoned. It has become an advocate. The proper role of the group in these circumstances cannot be sorted out in theories and hypotheticals. It involves some contradictions that are quite divisive in the NGO community, between justice and peace, for example, or the matter of when and how to cooperate with authoritarian rulers. The group can be a reporting vehicle, a monitor, a watchdog, a dissident, a conciliator, a mediator, an educator—but it can only be some of these things, not all. The most effective NGOs sort out what they can best bring to the table. Church-based groups may draw on the religious traditions as healers; a lawyers group might be more effective as advocates. The "platform" idea is merely a construct that encourages the qualities of adaptability; the harder choices about which tools are drawn from the toolbox are left to the practitioners in the field. That is one reason why finding great athletes—energetic, versatile people with good judgment—is indispensable to good grant making.

In many of the conflict-prevention projects I've seen, however, there appears to be one common deficiency: an excessive faith in the techniques of conflict resolution alone. In some respects it is the mirror image of those who regard military coercion as a panacea. All the workshops, dialogues, trainings, exchanges, mediations, et cetera, will not bring a durable peace if a public demand has not been mobilized. As a result, conflict prevention must be integrated with broader strategies of participation, empowerment, and the like, to provide an irresistible political force in which the more refined and subtle techniques of engagement can succeed. John Paul Lederach, perhaps, understands this better than anyone in the field, and he has grounded his entire theory and practice of "sustainable reconciliation" on the idea of mobilizing the indigenous in their own cultural and political context. The view that a transformation is to take place and be sustained over a long period of time, measured in decades, signals that the old ways of thinking about security issues—mainly militaristic, hegemonic views in which one group dominates and exerts its will by armed force—must be transformed if we are to avoid repeating ourselves, by, for example, "resolving" the same conflict over and over because the underlying structure of violence was never altered.[4] Burundi is a good example of where the conflict-resolvers understand that a public demand for peace is essential to moving the official peace process forward, and some of the NGOs there have actively promoted enlarged participation to express a desire for peace. It is noteworthy that the attempts to build public demands for peace are often engineered by women. Remember that the women of the Gold Medal Mothers' antiwar movement in the United States during the late 1960s and early 1970s were among the most effective protestors: Their boys died in a conflict they then openly decried, the most emotionally powerful appeal possible.

Visible and active concern about a war is at least two-tiered, however. The NGO practitioners of conflict resolution (the preferred term nowadays, incidentally, is "conflict transformation") often lament the lack of "political will" among the great powers to tackle the hard cases of conflict, which is certainly a frustration. Organizations like the International Crisis Group and the Forum on Early Warning and Early Response have been created in part to address this very thing, and both organizations have been rather effective. Too many in the conflict field, however, rely on the great white leader to come to the rescue. This noticeable error was focused on in a major study by the Carnegie Commission on Preventing Deadly Conflict, which constantly referred to the need for enlightened actions from the Western governments.[5] Emphasis should be just as sharply focused on building the political will inside the arena of conflict. A popular mandate for peace can alter the topography of concern, inside and out.

The link to public demands and social movements is crucial. As we saw in the case of the nuclear arms race and the Cold War, this pivotal ingredient was required to break the deadlock. Conflicts, "intractable" conflicts especially, persist because political elites perceive them to be sustainable and personally profitable. The examples of these types of conflicts are everywhere. When formidable public opposition to war is mounted, credible formulas for peace cannot easily be turned aside. If the public demand, over time, includes a critique of militarism and repression, the chances for a durable peace are enhanced. These demands face formidable obstacles, of course. But seeing the conflict-prevention toolkit as part of a broader social and political set of action repertoires makes the implements all the more effective when deployed.

For donors, this point is essential. For the nonspecialist, it is quite confusing to regard the array of groups and methods going to work on an incipient conflict. What good could they possibly do in such horrid conditions? The chances of some progress are far greater if the public is being mobilized in some fashion, however partially and fitfully, to express a popular will. With such a will effectively in play—not a small achievement, to be sure—political leaders will seek ways out. One can gauge the presence of social movements and public demands rather easily.

As to methods of conflict transformation, we were as a grantor rather ecumenical. Over time I became convinced that the historical dimension of conflict was being ignored by those focused mainly on mediation techniques, and this became our one, major theoretical focus. The need to delve into the "burdens of history," as Joseph Montville puts it, struck me as indispensable. History is often manipulated to serve fractious, sometimes violent, political ends, as it has been famously in the former Yugoslavia, but also in the India-Pakistan conflict, in Greek-Turkish standoffs, Balkans history more generally, in Northern Ireland, and many other venues. The past endures through intergenerational memory as a package of grievances and myths, politically potent if manipulated by unscrupulous leaders, and they cannot be vanquished by a clever negotiator promising economic rewards or rational argument. They must confronted directly, and the methods to do so include processes of self-revelation and hard, historical research culminating with the writing of a new, joint narrative. To this end, we funded major undertakings to look at U.S.–Iran relations, Turkish–Greek relations, and even some theory building, a rarity for us. The latter was a product of one of the great talents in the field, James Blight of Brown University, who developed an exceptionally dynamic method of "critical oral history," which combines history writing with meetings of decision makers from the period in question; a tangible outcome of the process is a form of reconciliation that I came to believe could be achieved in no other way. Like the link to a public demand for peace, the extent to which practitioners are willing to address the roots of conflict is a guide to the prospects for progress.

So we adopted these twin tracks on which to drive our program, the smart interventionist élan of the international NGOs, and the platform building of indigenous groups. We were mainly interested in proving concepts—experiments, in a sense—in places where some good could be accomplished, with the possibility that an abiding structure for peacemaking could be established. We gradually adopted some regional foci, including the former Yugoslavia, the Caucasus, central and west Africa, and Central America and Mexico. While results are difficult to quantify, I am certain that we contributed to that indispensable infrastructure of peace that can and has made a difference in these troubled areas. And we came to understand, once again, that the old Soviet Union must play a major part in our little drama.

THE NUCLEAR CONNECTION

By the mid-1990s, it was apparent that the problem of Russia's nuclear arsenal was not going away. The Duma was in the hands of reactionary communists or reactionary rightists, and they were not about to approve the second Strategic Arms Reduction Treaty (START II), or anything more daring. The command-and-control worries—the fear of nuclear weapons or materials being smuggled out, or weapons systems degrading and prone to accidents—continued to fester. As the Russian economy worsened, concern mounted over the consequences of not dedicating enough of the Russian government's budget to nuclear matters. While the Clinton administration had adeptly managed many aspects of the post-Soviet relationship, it could not control the deterioration of Russia's infrastructure, the leadership's willingness to comply with agreements, or indeed the Russian polity itself.

At the same time, the White House was determined to press for NATO expansion, which not only violated the agreement made when Gorbachev withdrew from Germany, but seemed foolhardy on nearly all counts. The Russians were reeling from their precipitous decline from superpower status. The bitter war in Chechnya, in which the army was nearly humiliated, fed Moscow's sense of vulnerability. The situation was disturbing not only because of Russia's possession of its enormous numbers of nuclear weapons, which was cause enough for alarm. Rather, the war in Chechnya and rumblings elsewhere raised the specter of Yugoslavia-like separatism that could make a mockery of Gorbachev's graceful devolution of Soviet power.

That perfervid nationalisms were a "new" problem of the post–Cold War world was quickly understood. The absence of communist repression and the globalization of economic and cultural activity were obvious sources of this retrenchment into group identities. But the deeply felt sense of grievance and betrayal was not due to the recent changes in rulers or trade, or the availability of "Seinfeld" on local television. Nationalism as a powerful social and political phenomenon had been unfolding for centuries, but its origins and meaning for the late twentieth century were underappreciated. "Nationalism is an inflamed condition of national consciousness which can be, and has on occasion been, some form of collective humiliation," Isaiah Berlin wrote thirty years ago, explaining its roots in the Germanic principalities of the Napoleonic period. "It may be that this happened in German lands because they had remained on the edges of the great renaissance of Western Europe. . . . To be the object of contempt or patronizing tolerance on the part of proud neighbors is one of the most traumatic experiences that individuals or societies can suffer. The response, as often as not, is pathological exaggeration of one's real or imaginary virtues, and resentment and hostility towards the proud, the happy, the successful." It is in this explanation that he traces the Romantic impulse that was a reaction against the Enlightenment—portentous for twentieth-century Germany, to be sure. "Certainly contemporary nationalism seldom comes in its pure, romantic form as it did in Italy or Poland or Hungary in the early nineteenth century, but it is connected far more closely with social and religious and economic grievances. Yet it seems undeniable that the central feeling is deeply nationalistic. More ominous still . . . , racial hatreds seem to be at the core of the most hideous expressions of violent collective emotion of this kind."[6]

The bitter and violent nationalisms that had riven Yugoslavia, upset the Caucasus and the Central Asia republics, and caused uprisings from Kurdistan to Chiapas—which mirrored, with remarkable fidelity, Berlin's observations—could infect Russia itself, with its hundreds of *petit* nations and clans, its deep sense of anger and shame over the collapse of its empire, its economic catastrophe. Far lesser cause has stirred massive genocides. The thought of Russia descending into such chaos, with nuclear weapons being wielded instead of machetes, was a vision of Hell itself.

From 1993 to 1996, our approach to the former Soviet Union was threefold. First was a long-standing commitment to help build the National Press Institute in Moscow. This arduously and meticulously constructed institute, a creation of the Center for War, Peace, and the News Media at NYU, provided training and resources for Russian journalists—a hands-on, information-rich environment that fosters a free press in Russia. This commitment, in our view, was a considerable achievement, due to the vision and hard work of the center's director, Robert Karl Manoff. Second was a decision in the early 1990s to work on building conflict-prevention capacity in the Caucasus, one of the most unstable corners of the old empire and, for us, a region of manageable size. Tara Magner developed this program, which mainly built infrastructure for NGOs to work in Armenia, Georgia, and Azerbaijan. With its new oil wealth, Russian meddling, and Islamic rebellion, the significance of the Caucasus is obvious. Third was our general work on nuclear disarmament, which included early support for public education in the United States on NATO expansion, which the Winston trustees in particular deemed to be a colossal mistake. We mounted a campaign to question the rush to include the old Warsaw Pact countries, a cause to which I recruited several other donors in an effort that lost the first round (Poland, Hungary, Czechia), but may have slowed the momentum to expand to Russia's borders.

But this program was clearly not enough to address the growing instability in Russia. Even as a small foundation, Winston had to address this instability more directly. Our funding on nuclear matters until 1996 had continued with a potpourri of concerns: U.S. export policy, nuclear secrecy, the plutonium cycle, proliferation in East Asia, and the nuclear test ban. The focus was not steady and the rationale was not compelling. The funding on NATO expansion might reduce external sources of instability, but the internal sources were really more worrisome. Tara Magner went to Russia to consult with NGOs and experts in Moscow, and we developed a funding program that we then funded with close to a million dollars over three years to promote more responsibility for the nuclear fuel cycle in the Russian Federation.

Such a program was brazen, to be sure. Our gamble was that because several other American donors were supporting the nurturing of expertise in Moscow, we should promote the growth of a grassroots movement in the countryside. But activists in places like Tomsk, Chelyabinsk, and Krasnoyarsk could not challenge the military over nuclear weapons policy directly; it was still too dangerous for such boldness. What the Russian NGOs could do, however, was to question the authorities and raise public awareness about nuclear safety and pollution. The nuclear facilities in the cities where such people were organizing were the pivot points of such organizing, and this tactic proved to be a useful way of going. Like the growing antinuclear sentiment of the early 1980s in the United States, the relationship among things nuclear, whether for defense or energy production, is blurry in the public's mind; in Russia, moreover, the wall between defense and energy is much lower than it is in the United States. And the 1986 accident at Chernobyl and reports of other sizable disasters of radiation releases made a strong impression on the Russian mind.

The grant-making focus mimicked our strategy of a decade earlier in the United States. We supported the best and most versatile groups, regardless of their precise issue emphasis. The leaders of the organizations were exceptionally skilled, knowledgeable, and experienced people—such as the indefatigable Lydia Popova, director of the Center for Nuclear Ecology and Energy Policy, who spent two decades in the Soviet Ministry of Atomic Power; or the physicist Alexey Yablokov, a Tolstoy-like character who was an adviser to Boris Yeltsin before he broke away to form the Center for Russian Environmental Policy. By creating strong, regional NGOs (or Moscow-based NGOs that supported the grassroots), I sensed we could mount a popular demand and force a new level of accountability on the Russian authorities. Of course, Russian democracy might be wholly dysfunctional, in which case just about any in-country funding strategy was doomed. To the extent that Russian leaders would respond to the concerns of their constituents, however, we had the chance of starting something quite significant in Russia. George Soros, the W. Alton Jones Foundation, and the Ploughshares Fund were also supporting many of the same groups. So the total amount of money flowing in to support this nuclear accountability work was enough to secure a place in the political culture, as long as Russia remained reasonably stable.

That latter concern was another spark for our funding. By establishing a few, strong, technically based organizations, we were contributing to the growth of civil society more broadly. Several of these organizations also worked on other public concerns, such as chemical pollution or biodiversity. Because they had a solid scientific grounding, they were by nature basing their legitimacy on universal principles rather than narrow ethnic or ideological claims, which was an immensely important pillar of an effective civil society. And it is civil society that may be the best hope for stabilizing Russia, providing a voice for ordinary people that is shorn of hypernationalism and economic corruption that now constitute the twin dangers to the Russian democratic experiment. Private philanthropy can do just so much in this respect, given the sheer scale of Russia and its problems—corruption in particular, which can distort international efforts. For all the hand-wringing about Russia, all the billions that were poured into the privatization of industry and stabilization of its currency (while, paradoxically, pouring billions into the expansion of NATO), the Western powers are paying a pittance for the great alkaline bath that is civil society. By the same reasoning, those who view the nuclear arsenal of Russia as the principal problem are again mistaking the symptoms for the disease.

CIVIL SOCIETY AND ITS DISCONTENTS

The agenda of preventive action advanced by civil society actors the world over barely appeared before it was attacked from several quarters. There was the bland assertion that this form of anticipatory work offered nothing new to diplomacy. Others argued that the possibility of preventing conflicts required exorbitant investments in places where the outcomes could be spoiled by a greedy ruler or miscalculation. Moreover, as one social scientist put it, "there is little basis for optimism in the ability of social science to precisely forecast the outbreak of violent domestic conflicts." He cited Bosnia, Rwanda, and Somalia as places where "prevention" (in the form of state actions) exacerbated the conflicts. Another critic—a freelance journalist—lampooned a meeting in Zagreb convened by the National Endowment for Democracy: "If this is dialogue worthy of Woody Allen's early, funny films, it is not far from the more sober faith of the rest of the donors: that by exchanging views in a frank and open manner in a fine hotel, even the bloodiest, most intractable harms of the world can be put right."[7] Books by Michael Maren (*The Road to Hell: The Ravaging Effects of Foreign Aid and International Charity*) and Thomas Carothers (*Assessing Democracy Assistance*) searingly upbraid foreign aid bumbling in Africa and Romania.

One cannot escape the impression that academics and journalists are lining up to take pot shots at NGOs. The most obvious reason for such actions is that civil society organizations present a new and formidable challenge to each institution's self-image as the prime interpreter of world events. For the news media—in an age of glamour obsessiveness and corporate domination of news outlets—the independence, moral stature, and on-the-ground *bona fides* of NGOs are perhaps too much to stomach. An editor at National Public Radio once came to me with a project for covering the growth of civil society organizations in Africa, and her proposal was to "expose" the self-dealing and corruption of these groups, which had somehow eluded me in viewing perhaps two hundred such NGOs over the previous five years or so. This editor's bizarre suggestion goes to the heart of the journalistic enterprise nowadays. Taking the conventional wisdom—for example, the civil society phenomenon as a good thing—and turning it on its head is a way to make one's bones in the fourth estate, and of course nothing else really matters except getting on page one. Academics grind a different axe. Having achieved creeping irrelevance in global affairs, scholars see NGOs as yet another layer distancing them from policy makers. (NGOs and academics are at times in competition for grant money as well.) Civil society actors tend to be real players, unsystematic, improvisational, and ethically committed—all qualities eschewed by academic standards. It is no wonder, then, that a small cottage industry in universities has grown to evaluate the performance of NGOs.

Political attacks have also been heavy. The right wing in America has for two decades assailed what neocon godfather Irving Kristol called "the new class," meaning the public interest groups advocating for cleaner environments, rights for women and minorities, disarmament, and so on. These leading lights of American civil society were viewed as nothing more than socialist stalking horses trying to slow down the dynamo of American capitalism. Foundations came under the same barrage of criticism when they supported such advocacy groups; a common complaint was that such activism did not jibe with the "original intent" of the robber baron donors. The right has even created a new institution, the Philanthropy Roundtable, to launch attacks on liberal philanthropy's misguided, "one world" philosophy.[8]

The left has joined in with similar criticisms. The vogue of civil society has apparently gotten under the skin of the old-fashioned statists. A representative attack comes from celebrity journalist David Rieff in *The Nation*. "When we put our faith in civil society, we are grasping at straws," he opened a 1999 essay. "The dogma holding that strengthening civil society is the key to creating or sustaining a healthy polity has come to dominate the thinking of major charitable foundations, as well as human rights and humanitarian organizations." What is especially nettlesome to Rieff is what he alleges is civil society organizations' role as playthings of international capitalism. "Far from being oppositional, [the idea of civil society] is perfectly in tune with . . . what might more unsentimentally be called 'Thatcherism with a human face,'" he charged. "The advocates of civil society are the useful idiots of globalization."[9] He goes on, among other errors, with the unattributed assertion that proponents of civil society believe it will replace the nasty old state and usher in a new dawn of civilization.

Much of the old left is bothered by the decline of strong states, which were long embraced as the provider of everything needed for a decent life. That civil society rose to prominence at the same time that the Soviet system collapsed makes NGOs a convenient target for these disappointed statists. What is particularly foolish in Rieff's essay is the idea that state and society must be in opposition; that is an accusation derived from Marx and used by the right for a hundred and fifty years. Much of the NGO activity we see today in many countries (and not just postcommunist regimes) is intended to strengthen the institutions of the public sphere—legal structures have gained particular attention—and the parallel institutions (*e.g.*, independent news media) that can keep states honest and accountable. Advocacy for debt relief, demilitarization, police reform, broadened education and health systems, protection of minorities, and dozens of other causes are done precisely to make government fairer, more efficient, and less likely to self-immolate. I know of no practitioner who thinks NGOs can or will replace states. (The origin of this idea seems to come from an essay by Jessica Mathews in *Foreign Affairs*.) Where civil society groups have played a large role in taking on the responsibilities of weak governments is in places where old centralized state systems, corrupt and inefficient as they nearly always are, collapsed and were rescued by the "international community" (more states) that then subcontracted to the only organizations capable or willing to do the hard work of rebuilding: the NGOs. Even where strong states are functioning reasonably well, they are prone to disaster precisely because they are so rigid: When a mistake is made, the brittle system cannot adapt and is thereby vulnerable. Consider Zimbabwe, long a success story and the kind of strong state in Africa that Rieff idolizes. When the AIDS crisis came to Africa, President Robert Mugabe denied its existence in Zimbabwe (not an uncommon reaction among political leaders). In the absence of a government program of prevention and treatment, the HIV infection rate in Zimbabwe is now at about 40 percent, possibly higher. It will destroy the country (if his policy to drive white farmers from their land does not destroy it first). The only organizations trying to respond are NGOs, against great odds. If the younger generation there survives intact, civil society will be its savior, not the strong state.

This example is not an isolated one—there are thousands of them. Strong states are particularly inflexible and prone to horrific ideological mistakes, which they then enforce with the instruments of state power—violence, mainly, or coercion or jail time or marginalization. A strong civil society is one of the only ways to enhance the state's responsiveness. It is also the best hedge against the ravages of "globalization." So where does Rieff think the movement to constrain free markets came from? Environmentalism, labor activists, cultural survival proponents, indigenous rights advocates—these are the forces trying to tame globalization, and they are the forces of civil society. The strong states (China comes to mind here) are lining up to sign on to unregulated markets.

In the real world, civil society organizations work with governments and international agencies to affect change, and I know of no NGO in the conflict field that has purposefully distanced itself from government. (Some do refuse any government funding, however.) Only the state or interstate organizations can militarily enforce a cease-fire, legally prosecute a war criminal, or pay for the immense costs of post-conflict reconstruction. Everyone in the field knows that, and no one would deny it. Everyone in the conflict-prevention arena welcomes states that are ready and willing to take strong action on behalf of peace.

The left should welcome the internationalist ideals and progressive values inherent in civil society. To describe this remarkable and hopeful phenomenon as part of a conspiracy of international capitalism is more than a perplexing lie; it is insidious and septic.

I go on at some length here with Rieff's essay because it represents a certain kind of left-wing thinking that begrudges the possibilities created within civil society. It's reminiscent of the leftist critics of conflict resolution, who angrily see mediation as a plot by corporations to muffle and defeat dissidents. This viewpoint is shortsighted. The number of tools available to civil society actors is enormous and varied, of which mediation is one. No community alerted and informed to the issues needs to compromise if viable alternatives exist. Conflict transformation techniques, seen as part of this much larger action menu, should be quite appealing to those averse to military force or economic coercion. And the same is true for the promise in civil society more generally.

What *is* questionable about the work of civil society organizations is their effectiveness. Here the waters get murky very quickly, because measuring effect in complex situations is immensely difficult. NGOs can embellish their claims of impact like anyone else. Some of the standard bromides—that any growth of civil society institutions contributes to stability, peace, accountability, and so on—are not reliable guides. Nor, as we've seen in the old Soviet empire, are American-style applications of electoral democracy or market-based economic reforms. Much foreign aid money from U.S. sources was geared to quick applications of such remedies, and NGOs were the vehicles of that policy. It's better understood today that a rapid transition to market economies, to cite the obvious, is not a sure route to stability. Some projects may be ahead of, or behind, the development curve of a particular political culture. Usually the worse that can happen is wasted money. But in some volatile places—Guatemala, Kenya, and Israel-Palestine are three examples—that have attracted an unusually large number of outside groups, legitimate concerns have surfaced about foreigners' meddling and stirring up more political dust than the system can absorb. Human rights organizations in particular seem impervious to the occasional need for nuance and sensitivity. But even here the criticisms may often be politically motivated (authorities irritated at being held accountable), and the impact is undeniable.

On a scale of intervention, in which one would rank international organizations, governments, corporations, NGOs, and scholars, my guess is that NGOs provide the best cost-benefit ratio. We know that there are many foolish and misbegotten projects by civil society actors. We know that even well-organized and administered NGO programs can fail to make a dent in a particular situation. We know that there are "bad" NGOs, typically created by competing political elites.[10] But all of these things are just as true of the other institutions, and there is considerably less potential for harmful impact with NGOs. In any case, the lines are not easily drawn in the workaday world of a conflict zone. A prominent relief organization that also provides, say, conflict management services in refugee camps may be headed by a former U.S. government official, be recruited for the specific assignment by a Scandinavian foreign ministry, be detailed to a UN agency for certain functions, be protected by a NATO task force, sit on an advisory group to the World Bank, advise a local government, raise large contributions from multinational corporations, and take donations of blankets and cans of food from a church network in Massachusetts. To which sector does it belong?

What we do know by now is that a large percentage of civil society groups, indigenous or international, have proven to be very effective in a wide range of settings.[11] They have some unique advantages over official bodies, which of course is not a claim to *replace* officialdom. They have developed sophisticated action repertoires that can be called upon for specific conditions, and they attract a high quality of talent. That we still can't measure effectiveness with much precision is not the same thing as saying that NGOs have no effect. What it does say is that we need to know more about what works and why. And the effort to answer such questions is certainly the province of philanthropy.

THE UNCERTAIN TRUMPET
OF AMERICAN PHILANTHROPY

Very few private foundations in the United States embraced conflict prevention after the Cold War. I attribute this lack to the fact that the international security donors were born in the nuclear cradle and never wanted to leave it. Nuclear arms control and the U.S. policy-making process are what they know, and it is difficult to take up something so new and different. At a donors meeting in April 1999, one program officer of a large foundation wondered aloud how one could possibly make good choices about such faraway conflicts as Rwanda or Chechnya or Sri Lanka. I answered that very few foundation people were trained formally in nuclear weapons issues, an immensely complex topic, yet we made decisions about this field, typically based on discussions with experts. Another funder decried our ability to judge effectiveness—indeed, questioned whether any of the conflict-prevention work had done any good—even as eighteen years of arms-control funding on the test ban, the Anti-Ballistic Missile Treaty, nonproliferation, and the like was crumbling all around her. A third person, when the topic of the Kosovo intervention was raised, said "we don't do Kosovo," echoing others' sentiments that the small ethnic conflicts of such tangential lands were not important to the big issues of international security, like Russia, China, India-Pakistan, and "weapons of mass destruction" generally. To this I said that Madeleine Albright probably thought Kosovo was a pretty big issue just then, involving as it did a potential genocide in the middle of Europe, a vitriolic reaction inside Russia, and U.S. and NATO "credibility," among other considerations; perhaps Burundi or Tajikistan do not merit such high-level attention, but it is, after all, where people are being killed. Peace donors should at least mull the possibility of working where peace does not exist. A final objection had to do with what one funder called "the authoritative allocation of values," by which she apparently meant that the closer one gets to the action, the more one has to worry about funder-driven errors based on our own, fallible sense of rights and wrongs. To this I would reply that choices are made all the time with enormous consequences, potentially, to do good or harm. One should not remove oneself from the arena of conflicts because one is worried that a decision may go awry. Someone is making those decisions, and it might as well be me. Making the choice to avert—to remain away from the conflict because of this concern—has an impact, too, and it is just as likely, and probably more likely, to make an inimical impact on matters of life and death. To invoke another sports metaphor, I say, "Give me the ball."

The fact is that all of these doubters are excellent donors, not least because they ask hard questions. But very few have committed to the civil society strategy. A few foundations have made that choice, however, and they have done impressive work. Prominent among these is the Hewlett Foundation, the creation of William Hewlett of Hewlett-Packard, whose large and growing foundation long had an international security dimension. Some arms-control funding was pursued in the mid-1980s, but the conflict resolution program was started shortly after the Gulf War. It followed a funding program concentrating on domestic dispute resolution; the international dimension was added as a response to the war, but it followed the contours of the domestic program pioneered by Roger Heyns, then Hewlett's president, who had known conflict-resolution pioneers like Herb Kelman and Kenneth Boulding at the University of Michigan thirty years earlier. The major grants went to fund theory centers at universities, including Kelman's program at Harvard and leading programs at George Mason University, Syracuse University, and the University of California. By the mid-1990s, Hewlett was one of the largest private donors in the international field, and had branched out to include some practitioners such as Search for Common Ground, Montville's program at the Center for Strategic and International Studies, and John Paul Lederach's work at Eastern Mennonite University. Throughout the 1990s, Hewlett combined its interest in theory-building with track two diplomacy. It is unusual in emphasizing long-term, general support grants, another legacy of Heyns. "The more I think about conflicts abroad," observes Stephen

Toben, the program head through the 1990s, "the more I am convinced that systematic, coordinated, long-term interventions are required, involving full-service agencies attentive not only to conflict dynamics, but to underlying political, social, and economic inequities that fuel antagonisms."

Hewlett's approach reflects to some degree the influence of its domestic program and a few of its favorite theorists, and hence a certain emphasis on mediation. Its willingness to fund empirical theory building—especially essential to a young field—and sizable, multiyear grants for core costs (administration and such that project grants will not pay for) has made it an exceptionally important player. It also has an eyes-wide-open view of political will. "We take isolationism in the Congress as a given," Toben says. "The notion of mobilizing governments to mount preventive interventions seems remote."

This approach contrasts rather sharply with another major donor in the field, the Carnegie Corporation, which graduated from "avoiding nuclear war" to "preventing deadly conflict" in the mid-1990s. The conclusions of the very expensive Commission on Preventing Deadly Conflict, the costs of which soared into the tens of millions of dollars, emphasized the mounting of political will among governments to take early actions that could avert war. A considerable amount of elite-institution funding—to Harvard and the Aspen Institute, to name two main recipients—also focused on the government links. "We work at the intersection of research and policy making," explains David Speedie, the program chair. He lists government-related programs as their finest achievements, such as the Nunn-Lugar legislation to fund Russian scientists (in the hope they would not migrate to Iraq, Libya, and the like), the congressional program at Aspen, which educates U.S. legislators, and a Harvard-based program that has engaged the Russian General Staff. Since David Hamburg retired in 1997, new president Vartan Gregorian has sent mixed signals about his intentions with the preventing deadly conflict program.

Intentionally or not, Carnegie's funding in a program for developing countries perhaps did more to build civil society and the kinds of NGO networks that contribute to stability. Much of this funding was for science and education in Africa, for example, and quite a bit of it was for in-country capacity building: $250,000 for a Forum for African Women Educationalists, several large grants to the African Academy of Sciences, and other major gifts for women's health issues. In this mode, Carnegie seemed to parallel the civil society effect of Ford Foundation grants, which long emphasized the nurturing of intellectual capacity in the Third World. Over time, Ford became more policy- and project-oriented in its poverty and population programs. It invests substantially in civic participation programs throughout the world, and its human rights and justice programs emphasize access to and strengthening of legal institutions. So while Ford's continuing emphasis on scholarship remains ample, and its direct investment in conflict prevention is relatively minor (*e.g.*, it has supported Search for Common Ground and the Communitá di Sant'Egidio), its sheer size—it was, until recently, the largest private foundation in America—makes its impact titanic. In the relevant program areas, it spends tens of millions of dollars annually. An approximately similar influence can be attributed to the MacArthur Foundation, which has no formal commitment to the conflict-prevention paradigm, but supports dozens of civil society initiatives and a few platforms for mediation, such as the Carter Center, Helsinki Citizens' Assembly (Prague), and the International Center on Conflict and Negotiation (Tbilisi). MacArthur conducts a most inventive population stabilization program as well, emphasizing women's empowerment and leadership, and such a program—while technically far from the universe of "security" issues—develops cadres of new, connected, progressive activists the world over, which directly contribute to the moral and operational strength of civil society and governance alike. Another dimension of this influence is the current security funding of the W. Alton Jones Foundation, which is entirely oriented to nuclear disarmament (and at more than $10 million a year), but has recognized that building relationships and the strength of NGOs in places like India and Russia is an indispensable route to secure societies.

It is in these ways that the giants of philanthropy make very profound contributions to the prevention effort, and quiet ones at that. They have as a group moved a long way in the last decade toward a more active, indigenously oriented funding profile emphasizing civil society and integrated concepts of global security.

The unquiet contributions are noteworthy, too, and one of them must figure prominently into any discussion of this field in 1990s: the George Soros phenomenon. Where a Ford or MacArthur might annually spend $20–30 million on projects enhancing civil society, and Hewlett and Winston spent $2–3 million each year in the late 1990s, Soros spent $360 million in 1996 and comparable amounts in other years. He created thirty in-country programs, mostly in the former Soviet sphere of Eastern and Central Europe. In many countries, the amount he spends rivals or surpasses U.S. foreign aid expenditures. His oft-noted philosophical bent is to support "open societies" in contrast to the repression of Soviet communism and other forms of tyranny. As a Hungarian émigré, his sentiments naturally inclined toward the "captive nations" of Europe.

"What the foundations have done is to change the way the transformation is brought about," he says of the postcommunist countries. "We try to choose projects that make a real difference. . . . our main priorities are education, civil society, law, the media, culture, libraries and the Internet." The Soros-funded foundations in the former Yugoslavia, the old Warsaw Pact countries, and the former Soviet Union itself have not only seeded innumerable projects in these realms, but are major players in the politics of their host countries, a fact that has caused considerable controversy in places like Serbia and Belarus. The projects range from the very large—a university in Budapest, a television network in Bosnia—to the very small. Improvisation and quick changes of direction have marked the Soros operation; one associate likened his philanthropic style to that of the consummate market trader he is. Like most dynamic systems that begin chaotically and gradually find a stable course, he acknowledges that "to operate without bureaucracy would render us wasteful and capricious. I have come to realize that we require a solid organization, a bureaucracy if you will. I have become reconciled to the fact that we must switch from a sprint to long distance running."[12]

The Soros philanthropies—the main operation is the Open Society Institute (OSI) in New York—have come in for their share of criticism, and not just from disgruntled autocrats. It is viewed as mercurial and often arrogant. The role of the OSI branches in the former Yugoslavia has been a lightning rod for criticism. Questions about whether they favored military intervention in the country, whether they had too much influence over U.S. aid decisions, whether they were too close to authoritarian rulers, were heard among the gossip. Their media choices looked wasteful and inconsistent. Applicants complained of favoritism, of a club of Soros beneficiaries that was hard to crack. The Soros offices in many Eastern European capitals, some charge, are run by the sons and daughters of the former communist elite. And there was opacity: What was he up to? What was his theory of change? "To open up closed societies, help make open societies more viable, and foster a critical mode of thinking," was his answer to the question of strategy. "Philanthropy is basically a corrupting influence; it corrupts not only the recipient, but also the giver, because people flatter him and never tell him the truth. . . . To protect itself from people who want to take, a foundation needs to be either very bureaucratic and have very strict rules, like the Ford Foundation or the state, or it should keep a low profile, working quietly in the background. I chose the latter alternative, you know: 'Don't call us; we'll call you.' "[13] But the problem was that it was not a low-profile operation—it flexed muscles to change policy in Washington and other capitals—but it still remained opaque.

The complaints about the Soros operations mirror those about other large foundations, for the most part, and are amplified by his high profile in the news media. What can certainly be said is that even his harshest critics (mainly the right-wing business press) acknowledge his good works, most of which are in fairly neutral areas of health, education, and culture. But the overall impact of Soros's astonishing binge of spending (which is due to decline early in the first decade of the twenty-first century) has been to stabilize those countries where he works through the provision of basic services (improving health care delivery, for example, or educational opportunity) and the overall effect on strengthening civic participation. The conflict-prevention paradigm, again, enters tangentially, as an afterthought, it seems, but is nonetheless real: The independent news media funding alone is a hedge against hypernationalist propaganda that is always an incendiary in these places.

Overall, then, the performance of American philanthropy in preventing conflict, building civil society, and fostering activism on behalf of progressive values is commendable, if incomplete. One obvious failure is the lack of consultation among donors. A few large foundations provide an enormous amount of the funding, which itself is often aimed to achieve other kinds of objectives. Apart from the Soros empire, the share of American dollars going to support these endeavors in zones of conflict is small compared with European governments, which are much more attuned to the prevention paradigm and have long embraced the links between economic development and conflict prevention. The U.S. government, through the Agency for International Development (AID), the National Endowment for Democracy, and the Institute of Peace, has also been a significant donor, though the objectives are more difficult to divine, particularly since AID (by far the largest player) traditionally has been an instrument of U.S. foreign policy objectives. But private donors from the United States nonetheless can play the leading-edge role that is very often the most appropriate and dynamic function of philanthropy-funding experiments, building empirical theory, seeding promising projects for the big donors, public and private, to sustain. The jury is still out on whether this uncoordinated, fitful attempt to create a global culture of peace and justice is succeeding. There are many reasons to question this success, in an age when globalization means we're creating two very separate and unequal worlds, one fabulously rich and safe and the other desperately poor and violent. But it is certainly worth the try.

10

MAKING THE MONEY SING

A man I met in South Africa a few years ago asked me what I did for a living. I said, as I have always answered the question, "I give away money." I went on to explain a little about philanthropy, about fielding proposals and making grants, and how we tried to affect the great issues of war and peace. That's ambitious, he said. Yes, it is ambitious, maybe even arrogant to think we can make a difference, I replied. With small resources and big problems, we had to choose wisely. And then he smiled and said, "You've got to make the money sing."

Money is not a static resource. It can be a burden, it can distort lives and ideas and projects. It can lure people into doing things they don't want to do. It can be like a leaden weight, bringing progress to a halt. It can make people too comfortable and even slothful. It can be lifeless. It can be stolen. But it can also be an instrument of remarkable, bold, exciting change. It is one among many resources, and it works only when combined with those others—intelligence, courage, hard work, solidarity, and vision. Its presence is neither absolutely necessary for change, nor does it guarantee change. Good donors recognize these qualities, that money alone is meaningless outside the context of how it is used. The best donors know that leveraging a little money to do a lot (and even the biggest donors have only a little compared with the scale of the world's problems) means they must find ways to utilize their resource with great flair and inventiveness. They must find a way to make the money sing.

How one finds this way—it's easier said than done, believe me— depends very much on how one thinks "getting things done" is achieved. Whatever field of philanthropy one engages, from preventing war to funding artists, the donor must have a clear idea of how using this precious substance of money will move people and institutions to do what needs doing. That is, they must have a strategy. Making a strategy is no more than being able to envision how and why the deployment of resources such as money, talent, technology, et cetera, will achieve certain results. This strategic vision must encompass the philanthropic enterprise itself: If the spirit of the operation encourages insight, risk-taking, and accountability, the more likely it will be a high-performance foundation.

The foundation community is a decorous place, a polite circle of well-educated people who are sensitive to their status as being among the world's elite. They not only get to spend lots of money, and be treated accordingly, but they're spending other people's money, for the most part, and this accentuates their elitism and remoteness. (The rich people I've known are always more down-to-earth and accessible than foundation presidents.) This social profile implies its own set of problems, but I take it as a given that most people suddenly thrust into this position would act much the same. An individual foundation officer or donor can choose to participate in that world, or take other paths. It is not an orderly universe. The current, "hot" issues of philanthropy reflect this lack of order. Should foundations be required to spend more than the legal requirement of five percent of assets? Many do. Shouldn't foundations put their money where their collective mouths are and invest in socially responsible enterprises rather than the stock market? Some of the stuffiest foundations are among the most progressive investors. There's no way to compel foundations to do much of anything they choose not to.

But what all donors *do* want is to be effective. The internal dynamics of this desire are pivotal. High-performance philanthropy begins with attitudes and ideas about how the foundation itself will operate. It also begins with attitudes about money—a timely matter, given the vast wealth created in the 1990s and the trillions now being transferred from the World War II generation to the baby boomers—and what truly satisfies a donor about philanthropic investments. And, in the end, high-performance philanthropy flows from a grounded theory of how social change occurs. If all these elements line up, then the money will sing.

THE "NEW" PHILANTHROPY OF THE NEW WEALTH

Early in 1998, several articles appeared in prominent periodicals featuring the newly wealthy of Silicon Valley who were getting into philanthropy. This long-awaited entry of computer megabucks was watched eagerly by all in the nonprofit world. Bill Gates aside, the money from the hundreds if not thousands of newly minted multimillionaires was looked upon as a natural for the liberal causes of philanthropy.

In explaining the reasons behind the formation of a group of prospective cyberphilanthropists on the West Coast, one electronics executive told *The New Yorker*, "The idea is to look at the giving away of money in a paradigm that people in our industry are used to looking at it—from a point of view where you can recognize budgets and deliverables." Another told the *Washington Post* that charities should recruit people who "know how to put together a business plan and demand results." The implication, of course, is that the established mechanisms for giving by individuals and foundations alike aren't demanding enough.

In the foundation world, however, the opposite is closer to the truth. Nothing more obsesses foundation officers than results. How to measure results, what in fact are good results, can results be expected in the short term—these questions are the daily dance partners of the grants officer. In the field of international security, "results" are most visible in reports published, conferences held, speeches given, or articles written. It is assumed, perhaps rightly, that those things are valuable enough in themselves to be accepted as good results. That thinking animates nonprofit organizations large and small, from the prestigious institute that offers handsome studies and intellect-packed seminars to the small advocacy group that promises that it will send every member of Congress a copy of its policy paper.

Such standard offerings look like results—"deliverables," in the idiom of Silicon Valley—but did any of it affect the conduct of war and peace? Did the organizations educate the movers and shakers in international policy making? A telling moment for me came early in my foundation career, when I asked a respected researcher to do an analysis of how Congress educated itself on defense issues. His conclusion, after extensively interviewing defense aides of members of key committees, was that the sources of information that were used most often—in fact, by an astounding margin—were the *New York Times* and the *Washington Post*. Studies, hearings, journal articles, newsletters, and seminars were very far down the list, virtually unacknowledged. I was left with the indelible image of a food chain from the think tanks to the seats of power that is long, entangled, and often broken, with very few nutrients making their way to the end.

Everyone in the business of making grants understands the problem. It may be that new generations of intellectuals and policy makers are trained in the bargain, but even that effect is far from certain. And the information age has compounded the difficulty, because the amount of data that is produced has grown significantly through faxed position papers and e-mailed newsletters, while the human eye can read no faster than it did a hundred years ago. Indeed, the glut of data and opinion makes the old type of "results" more suspect than ever.

Focusing on projects that produce such dubious results would all be harmless fun if they weren't diverting resources from other, less-conventional projects. As I noted in the last chapter, in conflict prevention the results are extremely hard to measure. The results of dialogues, new networks across old boundaries, growing toleration for differences, and the other practices of this new trade are elusive and sometimes ineffable. Measurements of success in American business and government tend toward quantification, which rarely captures the actual consequences of this kind of work. As one practitioner says, it's difficult to take credit for a war that didn't happen.

It is not surprising, then, that a number of grant makers spurn interest in this kind of activity precisely because they lack confidence in their ability to see "results." Instead, they tend to return to the more comfortable precincts of tangible products. That process, I suspect, is repeated in many of the fields that American philanthropy supports. But the search for "deliverables" is often misleading, and the desire for tangible outcomes often leads to grant making that is overly cautious. Ultimately, such attitudes starve innovation. We need to think of ways to demand productivity without relying on inappropriate standards. Beneficial results take time to unfold, and the perceptive grant maker must be able to appreciate that "unfolding" for what it is.

The image of the grant maker as entrepreneur, so often invoked among the new "dot.com" philanthropists as a longed for ideal, is not far from the current reality. We do make investments, mainly in people as well as ideas, and we hope to score a payoff. But the metaphor has been in fashion longer than desktop computers, and it's no longer of much use (possibly even less useful for people from an industry who scored their fabulous fortunes almost overnight). Social change is harder, more complex, and less certain than writing even a million lines of code.

The amount of thought that has already been invested into these questions could fill volumes, and much of it comes from people who bring different organizational skills to the table—again underlining the strength in diversity. To be sure, foundations should think more like venture capitalists in many respects, making certain that the core operations of an organization is healthy, for example, freeing the executives from fund-raising to concentrate on programs. Funders should allow time for projects to unfold. Funders should work with the grant recipients to maximize their organizational strengths and minimize their weaknesses. And so on. Some sensible advice is readily available on these matters, although too many foundations do not reexamine their practices routinely to enforce such practices. But the experiential base is there for philanthropy to exploit.[1]

This advice is relevant to the larger picture of wealth in America today and the underutilized place of philanthropy in that picture. The stock market expansion of the last twenty years has created mind-boggling wealth, hundreds of billionaires and thousands with money far greater than they could ever consume. The intergenerational transfer of wealth over the next two decades is estimated at many trillions of dollars. Giving has expanded, of course: In 1998, donations to the four hundred largest charities increased from 1997 by 16 percent overall, to $33 billion, although the gain of all charities was just 9 percent. (International groups in the four hundred, mostly geared to humanitarian relief, received $2.6 billion, up 13 percent.) That figure for the largest charities was the highest annual gain since 1991, when it was up 13 percent.[2] But compare that to the growth in the stock market, or to the estimates of transfers of inherited wealth. Consider, too, that poor people give larger percentages of their income to charity than the wealthy do. Or that the federal government no longer funds many essential services it once did, both here and abroad. Seen in the shadow of such questions, the philanthropic picture is not bright.

What will loosen the purse strings of America's wealthy is something that countless fund-raisers ponder as their daily work. Most fascinating to me is what attracts not just a steady, annual check of $20,000, but the committed innovator who can change history with his or her wealth. George Soros or Ted Turner have become deeply involved in substantive giving—donations well beyond the local symphony or hospital—out of concerns they long harbored about the fate of the world, but also because they find such activity to be deeply, personally gratifying. I saw Ted Turner at work on occasion, and the authenticity of his engagement was unmistakable. One biography of Soros describes his philanthropy as stemming from an expressive need, a midlife crisis of sorts.[3] Whatever the motivations, certainly very human emotions at work, they are models of action, highly charged particles in a universe of inert masses. They are people who *are* changing history, who have developed some ideas about how to do it and then put serious money into play. That must be immensely satisfying, far more than being a collector of fine art or a small contributor to hundreds of causes one cannot even remember at the end of the day.

That there aren't more people like Soros and Turner stems, I think, from the image of philanthropy and "good works" in popular culture. Charity is viewed still as the province of do-gooders. Philanthropy is equated with black-tie events in museums and Christmastide giving, and the large foundations make headlines mainly when a former college president is brought in to replace the previous, former college president. The pages of the *New York Times* or *Vanity Fair*, or the air time of Oprah or Charlie Rose carry only the rare story about NGOs or civil society or social movements. The social and political milieu to which the wealthy are exposed does not register what is actually occurring "out there," and the best one can hope for is that a fashion model or a movie star will take something up as their personal concern and bring attention to it, as Princess Diana did with land mines. Popular culture is not about to become meaningful, no matter what social-change funders do. But I believe there is some responsibility on the part of foundation executives, particularly among the larger philanthropies, to eschew the celebrity culture and help foster the alternative culture of authentic caring. This nourishing is done, but it is partial and timid.

One particular example comes to mind of this timidity. A meeting of international security donors was being held at a foundation in the Midwest. For a short time the president of the host institution sat in on our goings-on, and during that time I raised an issue that had long concerned me: I made an appeal for general-support funding for progressive news media. We had supported several, including radio programs, wire services, and magazines, that provided alternative viewpoints and, indeed, news with which the major carriers never bothered. I consider it essential to have such diversity in the marketplace of ideas, a market increasingly dominated by a few corporate giants peddling celebrity gossip. It also provides a way to connect people more to global concerns. Our host took umbrage at this suggestion, saying her board was "nonpartisan" and that they could not possibly do anything so clearly out-of-bounds. (She then made an impassioned plea, without a trace of irony, for us to write letters to the *New York Times*, which that very day had published a vitriolic attack on Joseph Rotblat, the co-founder of Pugwash who had just won the Nobel Peace Prize.) Today, several years later, the equivalent poverty of vision is evident in the foundation world's lack of investment in the Internet, the one truly hopeful phenomenon of technology in our time that is tailor-made for activism and civil society. Virtually no donors of the international security group are making grants to help create a progressive (which is to say, humane and universalist) presence on the World Wide Web, even as corporations rush to buy up and trivialize that medium, too.

If we cannot fearlessly cut a profile of caring, value-oriented, and dynamic leaders, we cannot expect the would-be Turner or Soros to be attracted to the world of international philanthropy. If we can't produce results that excite and galvanize, that say to the world, we are going to *do* rather than just criticize, we are going to *change* rather than just observe change, then we cannot expect to attract the kinds of people whose very existence as successful business people was predicated on dynamic doing. We can say, "We know how to change the course of history; don't you want to join us?" That is high performance, in the service of high ideals, and we are foolish not to present that face to the world.

This failure of vision and daring springs from the norms and protocols of most foundations, which cling to cloistered, insular habits of consultation and reflection, and rarely if ever challenge their own boards and staffs, much less anyone else's. It is world of ingratiating *politesse*, where no frank criticism is encouraged, where grantees cannot speak up, where the press never bothers to look. It is, in a word, unaccountable.

THE PHANTOM OF ACCOUNTABILITY

Private foundations actually have few formal responsibilities. There are strict rules governing certain aspects of their constitution, tax reporting, and prohibition from partisan political activity, but beyond that there are virtually no regulations. A foundation decides on its own how it will make decisions and to whom it feels any sense of obligation for its actions.

Observing how a few foundations make decisions reveals how elusive the notion of philanthropic accountability is. I worked for three different foundations—Winston, and two others I managed for a few years, the CarEth Foundation and the Henry P. Kendall Foundation, both in Boston. The three could not have been more different.

The CarEth Foundation was created by Sterling Grumman, one of the most progressive and visionary donors of the 1970s, among the few who supported protest during the Vietnam War. His legacy, CarEth (named after two aunts, Caroline and Ethel), was a small, family foundation that also had a few of Grumman's colleagues from the progressive community on the board. CarEth funded peace and social justice, emphasizing grassroots, racial justice, disarmament, and economic democracy. When we managed their operations from 1990 to 1994 (it's common for smaller foundations to share staff), the accent remained on peace activism, and we supported a range of organizations that mirrored the Winston Foundation's list but also emphasized CarEth's social-justice orientation. Most remarkable was the extraordinary care taken by each of the seven board members toward their decision-making responsibility. Grant recommendations, sometimes stemming from a board member's own circle of contacts, were thoroughly vetted at board meetings that often lasted two and half days (to spend just $150,000 annually). The board members belonged to a number of peace and justice organizations—SANE–Freeze, Fellowship of Reconciliation, and the like—and that kept them in touch with the peace movement. They read widely and shared their readings with others. Discussions at the board meetings were freewheeling and discursive, but always searching for the principled and effective action. It was a pleasure to work with such deeply committed people, whose own sense of accountability was unmistakable.

The process was quite different at the Kendall Foundation. The creation of an old New England family who made a fortune in medical supplies, the Kendall Foundation supported disarmament activism and had a large and innovative program in environmental protection. Robert Allen, its capable and visionary executive for eleven years, retired in 1987 and the Kendall Foundation went into a kind of hiatus for a short time; I was hired to return them to grant making. The board was all family: brothers John and Henry, sons of the sire, and a cousin. They did not actually function as a board, so the experience was much more like advising an individual donor. During my tenure, I dealt mainly with Henry, a truly extraordinary man. Born with the proverbial silver spoon in his mouth, Henry became a great adventurer, scaling the Himalayas, diving with Jacques Cousteau, piloting his own airplane. (He died at seventy-four while diving in Florida.) He was a world-class physicist, a professor at Massachusetts Institute of Technology, and a longtime leader of the Union of Concerned Scientists. In the early 1970s, he was one of the first to provide a technical critique of the safety of nuclear power plants—a bold thing to do in the clubby world of physics, earning him some ostracism—that led to reforms and possibly halted the growth of the industry. (It was a textbook case of a critical community feeding a growing social movement, and Henry was a towering critic—brilliant, insightful, and tenacious.) Early in his career he was a high-level consultant to the Defense Department, but became a prominent critic of nuclear weapons policies, particularly Star Wars. He shared the Nobel Prize in physics in 1990 (after which the National Academy of Sciences finally saw fit to invite him in).

Working for Henry was unique. Matching my own experience and knowledge with his was not a comforting prospect. He turned out to be quite a receptive donor, however, largely receptive to my strategy, in any case. His own ironic sensibility allowed him to deflate any Great Man of Science rigidity that afflicts some others I've known. But it was not a model of decision making. The absence of a working board, the sense of subjectiveness, the apparent aimlessness of the enterprise, and the suffocating effect of drifting along without a process of any discernable kind, all added up to a dispiriting experience. (These problems may have been temporary, because most of them have been significantly reversed by the present executive director.) Although I knew of Henry's deep commitment to the issues his philanthropy aided, there was no built-in mechanism, or any institutional meaning, of accountability. The potential for capriciousness in such cases is greatly amplified.

The Winston Foundation fell somewhere between the two polar opposites of CarEth and Kendall. The grant-making process was rather conventional: The staff recommended a dozen or two grants at three or four meetings annually, and the board approved nearly all, but provided comments that served as guidance for future cycles. The sense of responsibility and propriety on the board was very strong; one could see that from the care taken in starting the foundation, and I felt it every step of the way. Several of the trustees served on other boards, were executives of public interest organizations, or had been executive staff at major philanthropies. In these capacities, they were an exceptionally skilled collection of individuals. We had a reasonably clear set of objectives, but these were commitments to ideas and historical prospects rather than to a community of activists as such. Bob Scrivner's instructions were compelling but broad ("the permanent prevention of nuclear war"), and did not anticipate the end of the Cold War. To whom or to what, then, were we accountable?

Two different kinds of accountability are useful guides. The first is a constellation of people, institutions, ideas, and principles relating to *purpose*. The benefactor's intent is most compelling: It was his or her money, generosity, and vision that are the *sine qua non* of the enterprise. But the further in time one goes, the founder's gravitational pull weakens. In many cases, even in large foundations like MacArthur or Carnegie, the donor's intent was vague. So the benefactor's wishes lack durability and often lack clarity. Over time, the board and staff should nurture a vision and strategy, however, and this effectively substitutes for original intent. Visions and strategies are made up of people—the practitioners—and institutions, and they become the touchstone of accountability. That does not mean one accepts the norms and dominant ideas of that milieu—one can be "captured" by one's own grantees, in that the feedback loop of their community will, naturally enough, emphasize the urgency of the issues they work on—but injecting money into a field of work carries some responsibility for being well informed, fair minded, and positively inclined.

The second form of accountability is in *process*. What many people dislike about philanthropy is its secrecy, its clubbiness, and its opacity. Dozens of activists and researchers have remarked to me over the years that they could not get a clear sense of what foundations were interested in funding. Foundation officers were often remote, difficult to reach, and unresponsive. Grant guidelines were obtuse, too general, or constantly being revised. Grant requests were declined without an accompanying explanation. Even longtime grantees might be rejected and never told why. Several foundations will not even consider a grant request that was not solicited. And some funders are notorious for sitting on a proposal for a year or more without providing a clue as to its probable fate.

I sympathized with these plaints in part because I suffered, in a minor way, the same process. We managed in its final two years the award-winning periodical, *Nuclear Times*, and I had to raise some money to ensure that we could put out a high-quality publication. But I experienced a dismissive treatment from other foundations that was astounding. A major donor misled me about continuation of funding. Another colleague promised $50,000—a key to our taking responsibility for the magazine to begin with—and then she reneged, with no explanation. Others were reluctant to have an honest conversation about funding prospects. So I felt in one brief episode the slings and arrows of this outrage. Over the years I saw outstanding NGOs being shabbily treated time and again by foundations. I had vowed early on, and was gently prodded by my board, to have an open-door policy, to see anyone who legitimately fit into our guidelines. This policy was not just *noblesse oblige*; it was self-interest: many people who came to see us were much more impressive in person than their written proposals. It also enabled me to stay in touch with the field of work much more closely.

This openness is the essence of transparency, which is both a technical concept of how publicly visible a foundation's decision making is, and, more importantly, a spirit of engagement. When we talk about accountability in philanthropy, this is usually what's at stake. Pablo Eisenberg, one of the leading intellectuals of the nonprofit world, lays out a litany of problems with philanthropy, and nearly every one revolves around openness: "their failure to communicate with grantees, their lack of vision, the inflexibility of their bureaucratic structures and practices, their lack of performance standards and public accountability, their patterns of governance, and their overall relationships with actual and potential grantees."[4]

The windows of transparency can be constructed easily. It includes simple things like extensive discussion of funding priorities and decisions before and after a grant-making cycle; clear guidelines; willingness to meet to discuss an applicant's work; board members who are accessible to applicants, and so on. It's not terribly complex, and the effort required is not great. But too few foundations are willing to be open; instead, they are willfully resistant to altering the power relationship that comes with the money.

Accountability is also undermined by self-dealing, which is far too prevalent. I was told quite bluntly by the head of a major community fund that 10 percent of grants had to be reserved for board members' own favorite groups. A prominent Washington environmental grant maker spends 25 percent of its budget on a local museum so that one of the principal trustees will join its swanky board. A media celebrity is given the chair of a large East Coast philanthropy and proceeds to hire first his son-in-law and then his son as executive director. When people in the grantee community see these kinds of practices—and there are hundreds of them—they rightly conclude that foundations are prone to abuse their authority. The Council on Foundations and other such trade groups are unwilling to accept a role as whistle-blower, and the grantees are cowed by their need to raise money, which leaves virtually no mechanism for enforcing a strong sense of responsibility. "No foundation can evaluate itself, or its grants," says Karl Mathiasen, a leading nonprofit consultant who has belonged to several boards, including Winston's. "All are dissatisfied with evaluations in part because of unintended impact. Still, accountability derives totally from the board, from the extent of their engagement. At the New World Foundation, David Ramage was intent upon making the board, which included Hillary Clinton, live up to its responsibilities. They had to spend some time on the issues."

These issues are particularly germane during periods of rapid and fundamental change in a given field. The end of the Cold War certainly qualifies as that. When we began to reconsider our program, I spent several months talking to dozens of people in the international security world, including people we would never fund, such as scholars and journalists. I was suitably wary of the problem of "capture" by the people we had already been funding, which is a gravitational field that's hard to resist; one tends to want to justify past grant making by continuing along the same path, with the same people. But the end of the Cold War clearly signaled a need to look very skeptically at the old way of doing things. And healthy skepticism should be an instrument of accountability as well.

Few foundation officers feel that their processes measure up to some elusive standard of accountability, however. Boards are simply not interested in spending the time, and staffs are reluctant to mess with that arrangement. In the absence of monitoring from above or below, the staffs are rather autonomous. "Donors try to affect public policy, but who elected them?" asks Wade Greene, the Rockefeller family adviser. "It's hard to make a democratic case for private money affecting public policy. We challenge this in our own work on campaign finance. The major reasoning is that they're people with good values. But what about people with bad values?" Kennette Benedict of the MacArthur Foundation describes philanthropy as "a public trust," but that depends again on people of immaculate integrity. My own board president, Bevis Longstreth, asks "How do you measure effectiveness and whether you're doing something useful? You can put all the sunlight you can muster on foundations and still you don't know; the opportunities lost can't be measured. It's a particular problem of foundationland."

THE PAST AS PROLOGUE

We open the twenty-first century much as we opened the twentieth, with a strong, imperial, and self-confident America increasingly dominating the world economically but wary of any normative involvement apart from trade. Certainly, the fuel that fired the engines of imagination and activism twenty years ago scarcely exists: The "twilight struggle" is over, and with its demise went America's apparent interest in international politics. Many donors today believe this national languor is the great challenge before us, a twin to the spread of weapons of mass destruction, an apathy that rebounds against us.

As one sees Congress bludgeon foreign aid and undermine the United Nations, inflate Pentagon spending and slash budgets for global sustainability, defeat the nuclear test ban and then demand a nuclear missile shield, decry school shootings at home and pump up arms exports abroad, it is hard not to be discouraged. Clinton was an ineffective spokesman for internationalism, a Johnny-come-lately to the issue, so amid the perplexities of the post–Cold War world, the notion of principled engagement had no national interlocutor. It is a painful specter if one believes, as most foundations do, that the active participation of the U.S. government is needed to usher in a more humane world.

The answers for this disengagement in the 1990s were unconvincing, however, a panoply of committees for the United Nations. Most of the foundation money dedicated to redress America's growing isolationism went to the research centers and elite clubs to think about and discuss such issues. The appeals to the public, to arouse what is widely viewed as a latent internationalism, was done, if at all, through polling, focus groups, message framing, and liaisons with the major news media. The harder work of actually going to the people and working with them was left to the churches and a handful of humanitarian aid groups. (There is the sweet story of how an NGO, a local chapter of Bread for the World, stirred Alabama Republican congressman Spencer Backus to take the lead on Third World debt relief.) Social movements that already exist and have deep resonance with the public—those concerned with abusive labor practices in low-wage countries of the global South, for instance—are often bypassed in these efforts to "reengage" the public because they don't fit easily into the requisite image of cooperative citizen. Because these "antiglobalization" forces—another perfect example of a critical community aligned with a social movement—are so fundamentally at odds with the reigning paradigm of economic growth, they are rarely found in the salons of polite, international discourse. The churches find themselves in approximately the same position, though for different reasons. "Religious groups were able to connect to civil society through other religious organizations in the Middle East and elsewhere," explains Joe Volk, a longtime Quaker activist. "Funders did not see this as anything more than proselytizing 'church work,' which is not what they fund. The community orientation we have is not always understood by donors, who want a 'product.'" An in-depth strategy of mobilizing the public through secular channels would require a massive undertaking, a community-by-community effort at participation, possibly using the Swedish "study circles" method of education and action, to raise the consciousness of ordinary people about global issues. But that's harder than focus groups and bumper-sticker slogans and lunches with the media gatekeepers.

Of course, the American public is deeply engaged in international issues, but they express that through their participation in and financial support of NGOs who are active all over the world. That $2.6 billion figure cited earlier does not include the global activities of environmental groups, reproductive rights organizations, and many other smaller outfits, and it does not calculate the contributions of the churches and temples providing enormous sums of money and human resources around the world. The Agency for International Development (AID), while cut back in size in the 1990s, was essentially a Cold War instrument that was smartly reshaped by administrator Brian Atwood during his six-year tenure. One can safely assume that while AID's dollars totals are lower, they're being better spent than they were twenty years ago. The same is true of the World Bank and other large multilateral institutions. The news, in short, is not all that bad.

The worriers about American leadership also tend to forget that the national government is almost always going to act on behalf of national interests, whether defined in terms of security or economics, and that engagement is a very slippery slope when it comes to superpowers. Was not the bombing of Belgrade in the spring of 1999 an example of "engagement"? Is the World Trade Organization the quintessence of U.S.–led multilateralism?

For issues of war and peace at the beginning of the twenty-first century, the notion of the "indispensable nation" rings hollow. For environmental sustainability, perhaps, and fair action on trade and labor practices, one needs a U.S. commitment for action, because so much of the envisioned solutions are rooted in law and regulation. But even here, the "internationalism" can and does come from the civil society groups in the victimized areas. As in the conflict-prevention field, the flowering of civil society in the outback can and does reorient calculations in the major capitals. The influence of these social movements in the former Soviet sphere, Africa, Asia, and Latin America may not be as compelling as a powerful social movement banging on the doors of Washington, London, and Berlin, but it is creating a loud and persistent claim of control over these governments' people, in their lives, communities, and societies. Allied with the international NGOs, these movements and networks and intellectuals form the nucleus of a new internationalism, a new global wave of citizen activism. They are not only the "value guardians" of society, they are value revolutionaries in many places and social innovators virtually everywhere.

In this astonishing, worldwide revolution, there is not only reason for hope in its simplest form. It is in this civil society dynamism that we find the stories that can make correlations for the person watching the evening news at home and wondering what could possibly connect his life to the refugees, genocides, poverty, and the other dislocations that, every now and then, find their way into the major news media. The disconnection, the cognitive distancing that occurs between the First World of prosperity and the Third World of despair is not only a surface reflection of popular culture and news, but of the intellectual musings of Samuel Huntington, Robert Kaplan, Benjamin Barber, and many others. "If we put together the two narratives— globalization and chaos—it becomes apparent that we are not being offered a picture of the world that make sense," writes Michael Ignatieff, a leading thinker about these trends. "The absence of narratives of explanation is eroding the ethics of engagement. When all we see beyond our borders is chaos, the temptations of disgust become irresistible. If we could see a pattern in the chaos, or a chance of bringing some order here or there, the rationale for intervention and long-term ethical engagement would become plausible again."[5]

The narrative is there for the making. It is not only an assembly of stories about human courage and daring, invention and triumph, it is a paradigm of action and involvement. This narrative is what so much of America's intellectual elite have missed, reared as they have been on the notion that only major powers and great men make history. There is another narrative, one we can embrace not only as storytellers and interpreters, but as enablers and participants. The deeper the participation runs, from thinkers and doers (and funders) in America and Europe, to the thinkers and doers "out there" in the chaos, and back again, the deeper our solidarity and our sense of a shared destiny.

This moral cohabitation was, in a different time, the same one that animated the greatest achievements in American philanthropy as it confronted the problems of war and peace. In the early 1980s, the movements to end the nuclear arms race embraced this sense of a common future, a worldwide plight. The peasant in Peru and the shopkeeper in Bombay were as vulnerable to the nuclear madness as the Park Avenue set in New York. That these movements created a sense of solidarity is unmistakable. But the bonds did not arise from the ether of concern; they were organized and articulated by the critical communities and social movements in America and abroad. And supported, with money and personal involvement, by a coterie of donors who somehow saw the need for popular mobilization as a necessary condition of change. That was—and is—the most dynamic and effective aspiration for American philanthropy in war and peace.

NOTES

CHAPTER 1

1. Nicholas Lemann, "Citizen 501(c)(3)," *Atlantic Monthly* (February 1997). The left typically complains that foundations are too cautious and conservative, the right invariably the opposite, that they are social engineers and closet socialists. See, for example, Michael Shuman, "Why Progressive Foundations Give Too Little to Too Many," *The Nation* (12/19 January 1998), and Heather MacDonald, "The Billions of Dollars That Made Things Worse," *City Journal* (Fall 1996). All three articles are available on the World Wide Web.

2. I thank my friend Nick Bromell for alerting me to the Tappans. See Gerald Sorin, *The New York Abolitionists: A Case Study of Political Radicalism* (Greenwood Publishing, 1971).

3. Edward H. Berman, *The Influence of the Carnegie, Ford, and Rockefeller Foundations on American Foreign Policy: The Ideology of Philanthropy* (State University of New York Press, 1983), 3.

4. Mary Anna Culleton Colwell, *Private Foundations and Public Policy* (Garland Publishing, 1993), 68.

5. Alan Rabinowitz, *Social Change Philanthropy in America* (Quorum Books, 1990), 30. He used data collected by Independent Sector. The extrapolated figure for social-change strategies in the international arena, which is in cash, not time donated, matches up reasonably well with my own estimate based on adding up donations of the key donors we worked with in the 1980s in particular.

6. Thomas Rochon, *Culture Moves* (Princeton University Press, 1998), 8. There are many theories of social change, of course, but Rochon's work is highly integrative and, in my opinion, empirically satisfying. His work began with the peace movement in Europe in the 1980s in a case study, but in this volume he makes a comparative analysis with civil rights, feminism, and others of new social movements.

CHAPTER 2

1. All quotations that are not footnoted are from interviews conducted by the author between July 1999 and November 1999. In a few cases, the interviewee asked not to be identified.

153

CHAPTER 4

1. Quoted in William Leogrande, *Our Own Backyard: The United States in Central America, 1977–92* (University of North Carolina Press, 1998), 558.

2. Matthew C. Fellowes, "Public Opinion and American Foreign Policy: 1980–90" (July 1999), prepared for this book and available in full at <www. wf.org/opinion.htm>. All survey data, unless otherwise noted, is derived from Fellowes's excellent research.

3. Anthony Sampson, *Mandela: The Authorized Biography* (HarperCollins, 1999), 359–61. The official quoted was Frank Wisner, deputy secretary.

4. Eugene R. Wittkopf, *Faces of Internationalism: Public Opinion and American Foreign Policy* (Duke University Press, 1990), 74. The survey was the Chicago Council's quadrennial poll.

5. Matthew Evangelista, *Unarmed Forces: The Transnational Movement to End the Cold War* (Cornell University Press, 1999), and Raymond Garthoff, *The Great Transition: American-Soviet Relations and the End of the Cold War* (Brookings, 1994).

6. The *New York Times* quotations were, in order, from the op-ed pages of March 12, 1985 (Goldman); April 19 and July 21, 1985 (Simes), and March 5, 1986 (James Reston); *Washington Post* editorial, March 5, 1986; Robert Kaiser, "The Soviet Pretense," *Foreign Affairs* (Winter 1986–87). The last quotation in that paragraph is by Brian Crozier, "Gorbachev's Many Voices," *National Review* (May 3, 1985).

7. Deaver from interview with the author in David Cortright, *Peace Works: The Citizen's Role in Ending the Cold War* (Westview Press, 1993), 121. Cortright also cites Kaldor from her article in *The New Statesman* (March 18, 1987).

8. Barry M. Blechman, "The New Congressional Role in Arms Control," in Thomas Mann, ed., *A Question of Balance: The President, the Congress, and Foreign Policy* (Brookings, 1990), inter alia.

9. Fellowes, op. cit., 7.

10. Dana H. Allin, *Cold War Illusions: America, Europe, and Soviet Power, 1969–1989* (St. Martin's Press, 1994), 99. The speaker about "rubbish" was Richard Perle.

11. Garthoff, op. cit., 308, who cites an early 1987 White House paper "permeated by Cold War outlook" and with "no hint of recognition of Gorbachev's new thinking." Similarly, the right-wing press did not seem to know that their "strategy" was unfolding. A representative example by Robert Jastrow and James Frelk in *Policy Review* (Summer 1987): "The outlook for the next ten years is not promising. The congressional politics of missile defense—and especially the opposition to early deployment of a defense from prominent Members of Congress—are such that in the early 1990s the Soviet Union is likely to have a lethal combination of a first-strike attack force and a defense against retaliation—and the United States will have neither. In these circumstances, we believe it will be clear to all that the American government cannot protect its citizens from nuclear attack, and is no longer a nuclear superpower. The consequences, writes Robert Gates, deputy director of the CIA, will be 'awesomely negative for stability and peace.' We suggest that this development will be seen by the world as the greatest military reversal the United States has ever suffered, with catastrophic political consequences certain to follow."

12. Thomas R. Rochon, *Mobilizing for Peace* (Princeton University Press, 1988), 11. The powerful impact of the peace movement was apparent at the time, as several analysts noted. See, for example, my article, "Peace Community Is Now a Force," *Los Angeles Times* (September 24, 1987).

13. Arbatov quotation, cited in Evangelista, op. cit., 161. The social movements in the USSR were a beleaguered lot, to be sure, and some organizations were of state-origin, but they began to exert independent pressure for disarmament, such as the Semipalatinsk movement on nuclear testing. On the nonoffensive defense concepts, Evangelista provides the single best account, and the best researched, of how this process of influencing Gorbachev worked, but it was also a widely shared perception at the time. My article, "Demilitarizing Europe: It Takes Two Not to Tango," *The Nation* (April 17, 1989), drew from pioneering work by Joergen Dragsdahl, a Danish journalist, among others, in *Nuclear Times* and elsewhere. Some of this work is archived at <www.wf.org/nucleartimes.htm>.

14. Andrei Sakharov, *Memoirs* (Knopf, 1990), 617–19.

15. Evangelista, op. cit., 21.

CHAPTER 5

1. W. H. Ferry, letter to the author, August 27, 1987.

2. Thomas Rochon, "Three Faces of the Freeze: Arenas of Success & Failure," in D. Meyer and T. Rochon, eds., *Coalitions & Political Movements: The Lessons of the Nuclear Freeze* (Lynne Rienner, 1997), 166.

3. Kennan quoted in Rochon, ibid., 176.

CHAPTER 6

1. According to two nuclear experts, Stan Norris of NRDC and William Arkin of Greenpeace, between ten and twenty ships in the four U.S. carrier groups assigned to the gulf were armed with nuclear weapons. It is standard procedure to deploy nuclear weapons on the Tomahawk cruise missiles that are carried on those ships. Nuclear bombs were probably available to the F-18s on the carriers, and nuclear artillery shells may have been on the ground in Saudi Arabia. Perhaps five hundred or more U.S. nuclear weapons were integrated into Operation Desert Shield and Desert Storm.

2. Quoted in George Perkovich, "Think Again: Nuclear Proliferation," *Foreign Policy* (Fall 1998).

CHAPTER 7

1. Quoted by Stephen G. Greene, "For Programs in Peace and Security, a Reassessment," *Chronicle of Philanthropy* (February 12, 1991).

2. Ibid.

3. David Hamburg, *A Perspective of Carnegie Corporation's Program, 1983–1997* (Carnegie Corporation of New York, 1996), 21.

4. Quoted in Greene, op cit.

5. Waldemar A. Nielsen, *The Golden Donors: A New Anatomy of the Great Foundations* (E. P. Dutton, 1985), 141.

6. Stephen J. Del Rosso Jr., "The Insecure State," *Daedalus* (Spring 1995), 190.

7. A revealing, "Personal Report" by Frank von Hippel about his two years in the White House science adviser's office can be found in the Federation of American Scientists newsletter, available online on the World Wide Web at <http://fas.org>, March/April 1995.

CHAPTER 8

1. Lester M. Salamon and Helmut K. Anheier, "The Civil Society Sector," *Society* (January/February 1997), reprint, 1.

2. Jean L. Cohen and Andrew Arato, *Civil Society and Political Theory* (Massachusetts Institute of Technology Press, 1995), ix.

3. Quoted in Dennis Dalton, *Mahatma Gandhi: Nonviolent Power in Action* (Columbia University Press, 1993), 2. On his economic program, see "Resolution on Fundamental Rights and Economic Changes," in Dennis Dalton, ed., *M. K. Gandhi: Selected Writings* (Hackett Publishing Co., 1996), 101–2.

CHAPTER 9

1. Amos Oz, "The Peacemakers," *The New Yorker* (December 20, 1993), 77–85.

2. John Paul Lederach, *Building Peace: Sustainable Reconciliation in Divided Societies* (U.S. Institute of Peace Press, 1997), xvi.

3. For a description of Centro Demos, see George C. Biddle, "The 'DEMOS' in Democracy," on the Winston Foundation website at <www.wf.org>.

4. There are some theorists who are mindful of these sorts of problems besides Lederach; see Hugh Miall et al, *Contemporary Conflict Resolution* (Polity Press), 54–58, inter alia.

5. For a good discussion of the problems of early warning and political will, see John L. Davies and Ted Robert Gurr, eds., *Preventive Measures: Building Risk Assessment and Crisis Early Warning Systems* (Rowman & Littlefield, 1998). Consider just one comment from an essay (page 231) in the book, "Toward Response-Oriented Early Warning Analysis," by John G. Cockell, a Canadian official. " 'Political will' to act on early warning analysis is, no doubt, at least as important as the analysis itself. . . . But this handy phrase, most frequently employed by nongovernmental advocates to simultaneously blast governments and the United Nations while uncritically absolving themselves of any 'downstream' role, obscures complex realities at the policy and operational levels." For a critique of the Carnegie Commission, see my essay, "Forces of Civility," *Boston Review* (December 1998).

6. Isaiah Berlin, "The Bent Twig: On the Rise of Nationalism," in H. Hardy, ed., *The Crooked Timber of Humanity* (Princeton University Press, 1998), 245–46, 252.

7. Stephen John Stedman, "Alchemy for a New World Order," *Foreign Affairs* (May/June 1995), 16; and David Samuels, "At Play in the Fields of Oppression," *Harper's* (May 1995), 49.

8. One can view many examples of its hotly partisan attitude by looking at its archives at <http://www.philanthropyroundtable.org>; a particularly representative diatribe is an article by Devon Gaffney Cross and Frank Gaffney Jr., "Making Philanthropy Safe for the World," *Philanthropy* (September/October 1999). Among the Gaffney brother-sister team's assertions is reference to "conferences organized in recent months by the MacArthur and Henry B. Kendall [sic] Foundations to orchestrate the One World agenda." Anyone who attended those meetings would find this assertion laughable on several counts.

9. David Rieff, "The False Dawn of Civil Society," *The Nation* (February 22, 1999), inter alia.

10. A very useful discussion, based on empirical research in Kenya, on these points is provided by Stephen N. Ndegwa, *The Two Faces of Civil Society: NGOs and Politics in Africa* (Kumarian Press, 1996).

11. A helpful, short volume that addresses effectiveness, among other related matters, is Eftihia Voutira and Shaun A. Whishaw Brown, *Conflict Resolution: A Review of Some Non-Governmental Practices—'A Cautionary Tale'* (Nordiska Afrikainstitutet, 1995).

12. George Soros, *Soros on Soros: Staying Ahead of the Curve* (John Wiley & Sons, 1995) 123-24, 147.

13. Ibid., 113.

CHAPTER 10

1. An excellent roundup of these practices is found in Christine Letts, William P. Ryan, and Allen Grossman, *High Performance Nonprofit Organizations: Managing Upstream for Greater Impact* (John Wiley & Sons, 1999), 169–90.

2. "Raising the Roof," *Chronicle of Philanthropy* (November 4, 1999), 1, inter alia.

3. Robert Stone, *Soros: The Life, Times & Trading Secrets of the World's Greatest Investor* (Irwin Professional Publishing, 1996), inter alia.

4. *Chronicle of Philanthropy,* July 16, 1998.

5. Michael Ignatieff, *The Warrior's Honor: Ethnic War and the Modern Conscience* (Metropolitan Books, 1998), 98.

INDEX

ABOUT THE AUTHOR

For fourteen years, John Tirman was executive director of the Winston Foundation for World Peace—one of the leading philanthropies supporting peace activism. He also managed two other foundations and consulted widely in international affairs. He is the author of *Spoils of War: The Human Cost of America's Arms Trade* (1997) and is coauthor and editor of *The Fallacy of Star Wars* (1984), among several other books. He has written more than one hundred articles on global issues for periodicals such as *The Nation, Los Angeles Times, Boston Review, Chronicle of Philanthropy*, and the *Washington Post*. In 1999–2000, he served as Fulbright Senior Scholar in Cyprus.